N F T ™

Not For Tourists Guide to
MADRID

Get more on
notfortourists.com

Keep connected with:
Twitter:
twitter/notfortourists

Facebook:
facebook/notfortourists

iPhone App:
nftiphone.com

Not For Tourists Inc

Skyhorse Publishing

designed by:
Not For Tourists, Inc
NFT_{TM}**—Not For Tourists**_{TM} **Guide to Madrid**
www.notfortourists.com

Publisher	**Director**	**Graphic Design and**
Skyhorse Publishing	Stuart Farr	**Production**
		Charlotte Sunnen
Creative Direction &	**Managing Editor**	Federico Zuleta Rios
Information Design	Scott Sendrow	
Jane Pirone	Rob Tallia	**Information Systems**
Rob Tallia		**Manager**
Federico Zuleta Rios	**Writing and Editing**	Juan Molinari
	Julia Tena De La Nuez	
	Rob Tallia	

Printed in China
Print ISBN: 978-1-5107-2507-2 $14.99
Ebook ISBN: 978-1-5107-2518-8
ISSN 978-1-5107-2518-8
Copyright © 2017 by Not For Tourists, Inc.
1st Edition

Every effort has been made to ensure that the information in this book is as up-to-date as possible at press time. However, many details are liable to change—as we have learned. Not For Tourists cannot accept responsibility for any consequences arising from the use of this book.

Not For Tourists does not solicit individuals, organizations, or businesses for listings inclusion in our guides, nor do we accept payment for inclusion into the editorial portion of our book; the advertising sections, however, are exempt from this policy. We always welcome communications from anyone regarding ANYTHING having to do with our books; please visit us on our website at www.notfortourists.com for appropriate contact information.

www.skyhorsepublishing.com

10 9 8 7 6 5 4 3 2 1

Dear NFT User:

Greetings from Madrid! It's been awhile since we've produced a brand-new city, but what better place to start than the center of all good things Spanish? We absolutely love this city--its outdoor plazas, great parks, world-class museums, endless nightlife, and delicious food. But we most of all love this place for its people: the average Madrileño is more than happy to direct you to the nearest classic tapas joint, help you navigate the Byzantine rules at government offices, and, of course, join you at 2 a.m. for a nightcap in the city's most perfect neighborhood, Malasaña.

But Malasaña isn't the only great neighborhood in this city, not by a long shot, and that's why we decided to create a classic (yet newly-designed) NFT guide for it. Sipping a cocktail at the top of Mercado San Anton while you wait for Chueca's nightlife to take hold, wandering the ancient streets of Conde Duque in search of the city's most perfect record store, cozying up in a delicious tapas joint in Barrio de las Letras, exploring African and Indian cuisine in Lavapiés, window-shopping the latest high fashion in Salamanca, or simply observing the locals going about their day in La Latina, or Chamberí, or Argüelles, or any one of Madrid's dozens of neighborhoods, are some of our favorite pastimes here in Madrid, and we've created a guide to help you understand what it's like to live the life of a local.

And don't worry that this is all some esoteric exercise, either: all the obvious stuff is here too, since it's not just tourists who gaze in wonder at the El Boscos at the Prado or scream like maniacs during El Clásico. Trust us, there are plenty of locals in evidence, no matter where you go. Just take your NFT along to find the best stuff along the way; you'll be glad you did..

Jane, Rob, Julia, Scott & Craig

TABLE OF CONTENTS

NEIGHBORHOODS

Malasaña 8
Malasaña Map 10
Chueca 12
Chueca Map 14
Conde Duque 16
Conde Duque Map 18
Plaza Mayor & Opera 20
Plaza Mayor & Opera Map 22
Centro & Sol 24
Centro & Sol Map 26
Barrio de las Letras 28
Barrio de las Letras Map 30
Lavapiés & Embajadores 32
Lavapiés & Embajadores Map 34
La Latina 36
La Latina Map 38
Argüelles 40
Argüelles Map 42
Chamberí West 44
Chamberí West Map 46
Chamberí East 48
Chamberí East Map 50
Salamanca 52
Salamanca Map 54
El Retiro/Ibiza 56
El Retiro/Ibiza Map 58
Ríos Rosas 60
Ríos Rosas Map 62
Cuatro Caminos 64
Cuatro Caminos Map 66
El Viso/Castellana 68
El Viso/Castellana Map 70
Chamartín 72
Chamartín Map 74
Tetuán 76
Tetuán Map 78
Vicente Calderón 80
Vicente Calderón Map 82

TABLE OF CONTENTS

Arganzuela 84
Arganzuela Map 86

PARKS & PLACES

El Retiro 90
Casa de Campo 92
Parque del Oeste 94
Parque Berlín 96
Madrid Río 98
Estadio Wanda Metropolitano 100
Estadio Santiago Bernabéu 102
Caja Mágica 104

PRACTICAL INFORMATION

Calendar of Events 108
Estación de Atocha 120
Estación de Chamartín 122
Estación Príncipe Pío 124
Driving in Madrid 126
Metro de Madrid 128
Madrid Bus System 130
Aeropuerto Madrid-Barajas 132
RENFE/AVE 134
Cercanías Madrid 136

ARTS & ENTERTAINMENT

Museo del Prado 140
Museo Nacional Centro de Arte Reina Sofía 142
Museo Thyssen-Bornemisza 144
Museo Arqueológico Nacional 146
Museo Nacional de Ciencias Naturales 148
Museums 150
Bookstores 154
Theaters 158
Movie Theaters 162
Landmarks 164
Nightlife 168
Restaurants 172
Shopping 176

NEIGHBORHOODS
IN MADRID

Malasaña

Chueca

Conde Duque

Plaza Mayor & Opera

Centro & Sol

Barrio de las Letras

Lavapiés & Embajadores

La Latina

Argüelles

Chamberí West

Chamberí East

Salamanca

El Retiro/Ibiza

Ríos Rosas

Cuatro Caminos

El Viso/Castellana

Chamartín

Tetuán

Vicente Calderón

Arganzuela

MALASAÑA

PLAZA DOS DE MAYO

LA PESCADERÍA

FÁBRICA MARAVILLAS

Welcome to the center of the center! Malasaña is where it's at, folks--nightlife, cafes, restaurants, shopping, theater, live music, teeming plazas, and people still pounding canned Heinekens at 5:25 a.m. on a Saturday morning. While the rest of the world is commuting to work, the residents here (and, frankly, most of the rest of Madrid) are sleeping off the night before. When you do wake up, head to Plaza Colón, Plaza Juan Pujol, Plaza dos de Mayo, or Plaza Luna for some coffee and some tapas before a day of shopping on the busy Fuencarral. Poke your head into Museo Historia de Madrid or Museo National de Romanticismo for some high culture before some drinking and noshing at one of Madrid's classic bodegas, a short theater piece, some more drinking, some dinner, some more drinking....you get the idea.

MALASAÑA

LANDMARKS

1 Iglesia San Antonio de los Alemanes
Calle Puebla 22
Plain exterior, absolutely stunning
interior--worth the euro donation!

2 Mercado de San Ildefonso
Calle Fuencarral 57
Hip, buzzy night market for prepared
foods on three levels--delicious.

3 Mercado Municipal de Barceló
Calle Barceló 6
Giant 3-level mercado with dozens
of vendors-say hello to Marco.

4 Museo de Historia de Madrid
Calle Fuencarral 78
Fabulous entrance and overall great
museum explaining Madrid's history.

5 Plaza Dos de Mayo
Calle Daoiz & Calle de San Andrés
Where it all went down with the
French in 1808.

6 Plaza de Luna
Calle Luna & Calle Tedescos
Strange brutalist plaza with bizarre plaque
that can't be missed.

NIGHTLIFE

7 1862 Dry Bar
Calle del Pez 27
Perfect cocktails in one of Madrid's
most perfect cocktail bars. Enjoy.

8 Fábrica Maravillas
Calle de Valverde 29
Malasaña's own microbrewery, designed
to look like a Danish coffee shop. Bizarre.

9 Harvey's Cocktail Bar
Calle Fuencarral 70
Designed like a Vegas or L.A. lounge,
good drinks, decent food too.

10 The Stuyck Co
Calle Corredera Alta de San Pablo 33
Rotating menu of on-tap craft beers,
plus (of course) stuff to nosh on.

RESTAURANTS

10 La Bodega Ardosa
Calle Colón 13
The legendary Spanish bodega that's
almost always open (and crowded!).

11 La Pesacadería
Calle Ballesta 32
Delicious tapas, ceviche, fish and meats-
-try for a table outside.

12 Lateral Fuencarral
Calle Fuencarral 43
Perfect tapas and great outdoor tables to
rest your post-Fuencarral shopping feet.

13 La Fondue de Tell
Calle Divino Pastor 12
Cosy fondue and raclette in the heart
of Malasaña.

15 El Bosco
Calle Hortaleza 63
Fabulous modernist Italian tucked behind
the School of Architecture; a must.

16 Dionisios
Calle Augusto Figueroa 8
Perfect little Greek on pedestrian-only
Augusto Figueroa.

SHOPPING

17 J & J Books and Coffee
Calle Espíritu Santo 47
Books both in Spanish and English,
coffee, beer, and expats.

18 Generación X Puebla
Calle Puebla 15
Probably the hippest and biggest of
Malasaña's half-dozen comic book stores.

19 Viena Lacrem
Calle Sta Brigida 6
Best overall bakery in Malasaña...when
it's open, of course.

20 Panta Rhei
Calle Hernán Cortés 7
One of the best design bookstores
anywhere in Spain, and probably
Europe. Say hi.

CHUECA

FUNDACIÓN MAPFRE

TUK TUK

EL JUNCO

The heart of LGBT Madrid, Chueca parties long into the night. During the day, it's got the most famous shoe-shopping street in all of Spain (Calle Augusto Figueroa), perhaps the best mercado in Madrid (Mercado San Antón), and lots of little squares, including Plaza de Chueca, Plaza del Rey, Plaza Santa Bárbara, and Plaza Vazquez de Mella, to have a tinto de verano in while you wait for the shops to re-open. On the east (Recoletos) side of the neighborhood, the Fundación MAPFRE is a must-see, and more fabulous shopping is on tap along Calle Fernando VI and environs. Don't miss the ornate, Gaudi-ish Society of Spanish Writers and Editors Building while waiting for Chueca's best live music club, El Junco, to finally open (hey, it's Madrid--did you think anything was happening before midnight?). A nightcap at classic Taberna de Ángel Sierra is, of course, not to be missed.

EL BIERZO

TONY2

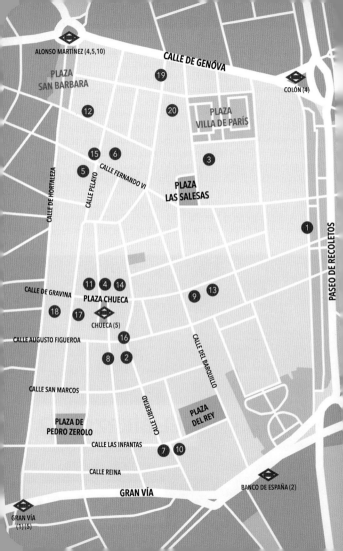

CHUECA

LANDMARKS

1 Fundación MAPFRE
Paseo de Recoletos 23
Brilliant, rotating art exhibitions-
everything from Italian Futurism to
modern photography.

2 Mercado San Antón
Calle de Augusto Figueroa 24B
Best mercado in Madrid--1 floor vendors,
1 floor tapas, 1 floor rooftop bar.

3 Parroquia de Santa Bárbara
Calle del Gral. Castaños 2
Looks like an amazing church from
the outside....sadly, almost never open.

4 Plaza de Chueca
Sit down and watch the neighborhood
move by you (or, more likely, sit and
drink with you).

5 Society of Spanish Writers and Editors
Calle Fernando VI 4
Brilliant Gaudi-esque modernist
masterpiece by José Grases Riera.

RESTAURANTS

6 Krachai
Calle Fernando VI 11
Very good Thai in the heart of Chueca's
hip shopping streets.

7 Paella de la Reina 39
Calle Reina 39
Classic Valencian paella, but don't miss
the black rice and the fideos, either.

8 El Bierzo
Calle de Barbieri 16
Traditional Spanish food at a really
good price.

9 Tuk Tuk
Calle del Barquillo 26
Great mix of Asian street food options,
especially the Char Siu and the Rendang.

10 Yakitoro by Chicote
Calle Reina 41
Skewered Japanese goodness, plus fabu-
lous marrow and a great drink selection.

NIGHTLIFE

11 D'Mystic
Calle de Gravina 5
Perfect Madrid cocktail bar for before
and after additional Chueca adventures.

12 El Junco
Plaza de Sta. Barbara 10
Head over at midnight for some of
Madrid's best live bands, especially
Thursday's "Black Jam."

13 Tony2
Calle del Almirante 9
Only if you feel like singing karaoke next
to a grand piano surrounded by drunk
Spanish people.

14 Taberna de Ángel Sierra
Calle de Gravina 11
Classic Madrid bar that you need to
drink a beer in, sometime.

SHOPPING

15 Cacto
Calle Fernando VI 7
For all your cactus needs. No, really.
Seriously. A cactus store.

16 Calle de Augusto Figueroa
Between Hortaleza and Barbieri.
A dozen shoe shops in a four-block
stretch: paradise!

17 Nakama Lib
Calle Pelayo 22
Lovely little bookshop with great
selection of Madrid-centric books.

18 Papelería Cámara
Calle de Hortaleza 68
Fantastic paper and art shop for
your inner Zóbel.

19 Poncelet
Calle Argensola 27
A veritable cathedral of cheese for
your gustatory pleasure.

20 Sugar Factory Madrid
Calle Argensola 27
Delectable pastry shop with the
best croissants in Madrid.

CONDE DUQUE

JACK PERCOCA

MUSEO ABC ◉

There's a feel to this neighborhood that's inescapable--a feel of true medievalism. You just kind of have to walk around the streets here and you'll understand what we're talking about. Yes, the shops and the mercados and the restaurants and the bars and the cultural institutions (such as the Conde Duque Cultural Center and the Museo ABC) are all buzzing with Madrileños (and with fewer tourists than other neighborhoods), but there are plenty of streets around here, both during the day and at night, that can seem pretty empty--in the best and spookiest kind of way. The shuttered Edificio España, possibly the largest current empty building in all of Spain, adds to the sense of oddness. But, just like the rest of Madrid, you can relax at a plaza (try Cristino Martos) sipping coffee and watching the children play while you wait for the clubs (try Tempo Club) to open.

PALMA BREW

LA CARBONERA

CONDE DUQUE

LANDMARKS

Centro Conde Duque
Calle Conde Duque
Brilliant cultural institution with fabulous rotating art shows and great live music.

Mercado de los Mostenses
Plaza Mostenses 1
Bustling mercado that features a good supply of Asian greens and sundries.

Iglesia de Nuestra Señora de Montserrat
Calle San Bernardo 79
Baroque church on bustling San Bernardo that's worth a peek inside.

Museo ABC
Calle Amaniel 29
Excellent museum of drawing and illustration with a super-cool exterior and kids' programs.

Parroquia de San Marcos
Calle San Leónardo 10
Conde Duque's best church, with an amazing floor plan and ceilings.

NIGHTLIFE

6 Bodegas El Maño
Calle de la Palma 64
Hundred-year-old bodega serves up drinks late into the night. Ah, Madrid.

7 El Jardín Secreto
Calle Conde Duque 2
Yes, it's a restaurant, but the decor is trippy enough for, well, you know…

8 Jack Percoca
Calle Conde Duque 14
It's a little bit of everything. Including cocktails.

9 Palma Brew
Calle de la Palma 50
Cool beer shop with (what else?) in-store tastings.

10 Tempo Club
Calle Duque de Osuna 8
Hippest spot in the 'Duque. Live music, DJs, stiff drinks.

RESTAURANTS

11 Esfahan
Calle San Bernadino 1
Persian goodness in the heart of Conde Duque. Yum.

12 Goiko Grill
Calle de la Princesa 26
Hungry after a movie? Grab a delicious burger. And fries.

13 La Carbonera
Calle Bernardo López García 11
Cheese and tapas bar. Did we mention cheese?

14 Meson O'Luar
Calle San Bernardo 17
Eat classic Spanish tapas with the hotel workers and cab drivers of Madrid. Perfect.

15 Restaurante Peruano Chincha
Plaza Mostenses 3
Good selection of Peruvian specialties and, of course, Cusqueña beer.

SHOPPING

16 Atticus Finch
Calle de la Palma 78
Best name for a bookstore ever, we think.

17 Headbanger Rare Guitars
Calle de la Palma 73
Channel your inner Jimmy Page (if you've got the budget).

18 Pescadería Gonzalo González
Calle Noviciado 9
Great local fish shop if you don't want to deal with the madness of the mercado.

19 Radio City
Calle Conde Duque 14
Best record shop in Madrid, hands-down. Say hello.

20 Supermercado Intertropico
Calle de los Reyes 17
Supermarket favorites from all over Central and South America. Impressive.

PLAZA MAYOR & OPERA

ASADOR REAL

TEATRO REAL

LOS AMIGOS

EL PIMIENTO VERDE

One of a trio of neighborhoods south of the Gran Vía that makes up Madrid's "center," this 'nabe has some of the city's biggest tourist attractions, including the Palace (absolutely amazing), the Opera (absolutely sublime), the Mercado San Miguel (absolutely essential), and the Plaza Mayor (absolutely overrun with tourist nonsense, but essential nonetheless). The beautiful gardens of the Plaza de Oriente, on the Palace's eastern flank, and the Jardines de Sabatini, on the Palace's northern side, are also not to be missed. In terms of classic Madrid shops and restaurants, it seems there is at least one down every street here; walking around will give you delight after delight, including the roast pork (cuchinillo asado) at Asado Real and the monkfish (rape) at El Pimiento Verde. At night, many of the tourists melt away from the western area; chill out with the few locals at Plaza Ramales and reflect on all you've seen.

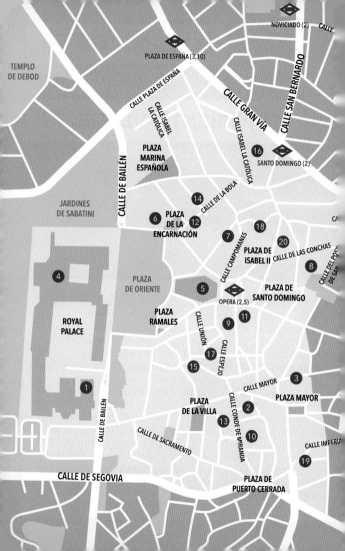

LANDMARKS

Catedral de la Almudena
Calle de Bailén 10
Whacked-out pseudo-modernist cathedral that's one million times nicer on the inside.

Mercado de San Miguel
Plaza de San Miguel
Jammed, but filled with delicious tapas and drinks of all kinds, in all directions.

Plaza Mayor
Barren, cold, devoid of greenery, filled with tourist nonsense, but still a must; the northern side is lovely.

Royal Palace of Madrid
Calle de Bailén
Giant monument to excess with some absolutely stunning period rooms and gorgeous baroque chapel.

Teatro Real
Plaza de Isabel II
Plaza de Isabel II. A lovely experience inside, a bit brutalist on the outside; either way, another must-see.

SHOPPING

6 **Alambique Tienda y Escuela de Cocina**
Plaza de la Encarnación 2
Great kitchen store, with classes too.

7 **Desperate Literature**
Calle Campomanes 13
Fantastic used bookstore with readings and hangouts.

8 **Discos La Metralleta**
Calle del Postigo de San Martín 1
Madrid's classic schizophrenic underground record shop; hard to find!

9 **Santa Eulalia**
Calle Espejo 12
Absolutely delectable bakeshop in a hip space. Nice one.

10 **Taller Puntera S.L.**
Plaza Conde de Barajas 4
You've heard of Spanish leather? This is where to get it. Just lovely.

RESTAURANTS

11 **Asador Real**
Plaza de Isabel II
For all your roasted cochinillo and cordero, in a classic space. Yum.

12 **El Mollette**
Calle de la Bola 4
Friendly tapas, especially buzzy at lunch (2-4 pm, of course).

13 **El Pimiento Verde**
Calle Conde de Miranda 4
Escape the madness of the Mercado and eat fabulous rape (monkfish) and artichokes.

14 **La Bola**
Calle de la Bola 5
Classic Madrid eatery that feels like home; try the house soup and gambas a la plancha.

15 **La Gastroteca de Santiago**
Plazuela de Santiago 1
Delicious Michelin-recommended dining on a cute plazuela..

16 **Vietnam Mekong**
Calle Isabel la Católica 11
Friendly cheap Vietnamese escape just a few steps from the Gran Vía.

NIGHTLIFE

17 **Anticafé**
Calle Unión 2
A little bit of everything, but that includes alcohol.

18 **Beer Station**
Cuesta Santo Domingo 22
We know what pulls into this station, and we're taking that train.

19 **The Hat Madrid**
Calle Imperial 9
Super-cool top floor bar of the Hat Hotel. No bling, just cool.

20 **Los Amigos**
Calle de las Conchas 6
Wanna go drink with the locals? Here 'tis.

CENTRO
& SOL

KILLER'S DISCOS

CASA PATAS

LATERAL SANTA ANA

Tourist madness, wall-to-wall. Plus, more El Corte Ingles outlets than you can shake a stick at, a huge FNAC electronics store, an incredibly ornate Casino, churches, underground music clubs, Ministries, hotels, and more shopping than you'd be able to do in your lifetime. We'd love to be able to say, "there's this little secret corner of this neighborhood where you can relax away from the crowds..."but there isn't one. Hence the name "Centro," with everyone and their uncle hanging out in Puerto del Sol at least for 5 minutes every day, for some reason or other. However, the nicest spot is easily the area around Plaza Santa Ana and Plaza Ángel, in front of the stunning Reina Victoria Hotel. Nearby? Great jazz at art deco Café Central (one of the best places in the world to see jazz, really) and delicious churros from Maestro Churrero. Just don't expect solitude.

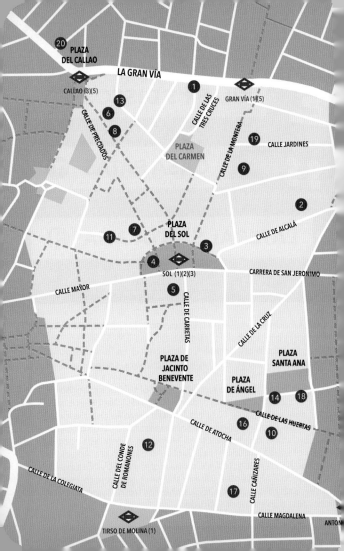

LANDMARKS

Calle Gran Vía
The street of streets. Filled with brilliant architecture and an unconscionable number of tourists.

Casino de Madrid
Calle de Alcalá 15
Yup, this is what we consider the best churros in Madrid.

El Oso y el Madroño
Madrid's symbol!

Puerta del Sol
Wall-to-wall tourists attempting to figure out where they want to go next, but still an essential stop.

Real Casa de Correos
Plaza Puerta del Sol
The best building to gaze up at in the plaza. 'Nuff said.

SHOPPING

El Corte Inglés [part 1]
Plaza del Callao 2
One half of the mothership--everything except clothes.

El Corte Inglés [part 2]
Calle de Preciados 3
The other half--clothes, toys, extensive basement grocery store.

FNAC
Calle de Preciados 28
French electronics giant's giant store just south of the Gran Vía.

Killer's Discos
Calle de la Montera 28
As opposed to discs for killers. Try it.

Ojalá Madrid
Calle de las Huertas 5
Great women's clothes nearby other good shops, too.

RESTAURANTS

11 Chocolatería San Ginés
Pasadizo de San Ginés 5
Madrid's most iconic chocolatería, open 24 hours. The place to go after a night of partying.

12 Café del Patio
Calle del Conde de Romanones 5
Friendly, a little bit of everything.

13 Gourmet Experience
Plaza del Callao 2
9th-floor eatery of the El Corte Ingles, with killer views.

14 Lateral Santa Ana
Plaza Sta. Ana 12
Central location of one of Madrid's best small chain of delicious tapas joints.

15 Ateneo
Calle de Santa Catalina 10
Dress-up Spanish restaurant located in the historic literary building Ateneo de Madrid.

NIGHTLIFE

16 Café Central
Plaza del Ángel 10
One of the best venues for jazz in the entire solar system, hands-down.

17 Casa Patas
Calle Cañizares 10
Super-fun, super-classic spot to experience flamenco. A must.

18 Cervecería Alemana
Plaza Sta. Ana 6
Because beer from Germany tastes good, no matter where you are.

19 El Sol
Calle Jardínes 3
Madrid's most classic of all its classic rock clubs. Nice one.

20 Independance Club
Plaza del Callao 4
If you enjoy classic rock music, this is the nightclub for you. Also your chance to discover some Spanish rock.

BARRIO DE LAS LETRAS

MUSEO REINA SOFÍA ◉

CAIXA FORUM ◉

EL ALAMBIQUE

Las Letras: the soul of literary Madrid. Also pretty much the soul of everything else, too--given the fact that three of Madrid's greatest art destinations (the Reina, the Thyssen, and the Caixa Forum) all fall within its borders, and that the 'nabe' is crawling with great old (and new) eateries, clubs, shops, etc. Even the Spanish government gets into the act, when it actually is functional enough to meet (which isn't very often, admittedly). None of this is a secret, of course, as two of the main streets--Calle de Cervantes and Calle de Lope de Vega--are named after two of Spain's literary giants. And the streets in Las Letras are some of its greatest assets--exploring the uber-narrow passageways of Calle de las Huertas, Calle Echegaray, and Plaza de Matute (which also has some of the best architecture in the neighborhood) is one of the best things you can (and should!) do here.

THE WESTIN PALACE

LA VENENCIA

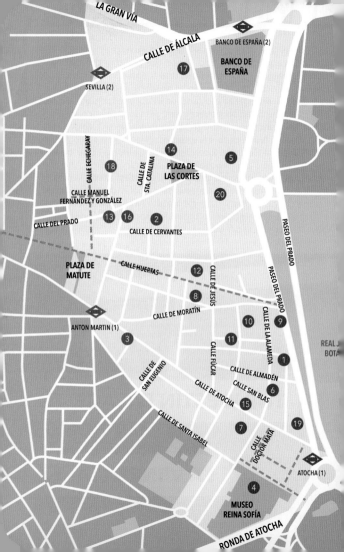

BARRIO DE LAS LETRAS

LANDMARKS

Caixa Forum
Paseo del Prado 36
Amazing green wall on the outside, fabulous rotating exhibitions on the inside.

Casa Museo Lope de Vega
Calle de Cervantes 11
Pay homage to one of Spain's literary giants.

Mercado de Anton Martin
Calle de Santa Isabel 5
Bustling as all other mercados, great beer shop inside.

Museo Nacional Centro de Arte Reina Sofía
Calle de Santa Isabel 52
One pillar of Madrid's triumvirate of world-class museums; this is the modern stuff.

Museo Thyssen-Bornemisza
Paseo del Prado 8
Another pillar, and possibly the world's greatest privately-held collections of paintings.

SHOPPING

Be Hoppy
Calle de Almadén 18
Cute little beer store featuring Spain's ever-burgeoning craft beer scene.

Guitarras de Luthier
Calle Doctor Mata 1
Drop-dead gorgeous Spanish guitar store; drool-worthy.

Indigo 50
Calle de Moratín 29
French electronics giant's giant store just south of the Gran Vía.

Papelería Losada Librería Artes Gráficas
Calle de la Alameda 3
Papers and supplies for all those artists who can't afford Las Letras.

Passage Privé
Calle de San Pedro 8
Antiques, furniture, gifts...just another cool store in Las Letras.

RESTAURANTS

11 **El Alambique**
Calle Fúcar 7
Seemingly small bar hides big flavors served up in the back room. Mmmm... Argentine steak.

12 **La Anchoita**
Calle de Jesús 4
Amazing little seafood-centric bodega with some of the coolest bar taps you'll ever see.

13 **El Lacón**
Calle Manuel Fernández y González 8
Classic Las Letras spot, love the decor as well.

14 **El Rincón de Esteban**
Calle de San Blas 4
Perfect place for Spanish classic. Enjoy.

15 **La Bodega de los Secretos**
Calle de San Blas 4
The secret is out; delicious.

16 **Lamucca de Prado**
Calle del Prado 16
Las Letras location of Madrid mini-chain; always dependable.

NIGHTLIFE

17 **Azotea del Círculo**
Calle de Alcalá 42
See Madrid (especially the east) from the top of this awesome rooftop bar.

18 **La Venencia**
Calle Echegaray 7
Old-timey bar on a narrow street--what can be bad?

19 **Teatro Kapital**
Calle de Atocha 125
Madrid's biggest nightclub: it only has seven floors.

20 **The Westin Palace**
Plaza de las Cortes 7
Have a cocktail under one of the most amazing glass atrium roofs you'll ever see.

LAVAPIÉS & EMBAJADORES

GAU CAFE 🍸

EL GATO VERDE 🍸

EL RASTRO ◉

Welcome to the heart of immigrant Madrid--or at least one of them, anyway. The rich flavors of Senegalese and Indian spices and cooking seep out of the cafes and stores here, while the murals and the re-purposed buildings (such as the Hermitage of the Pillar, now UNED's library and a roof-top bar, and the Tabacalera, a former tobacco factory, now home to dozens of official, semi-official, and decidedly un-official arts organizations) lend far more than just a passing "artsy" flavor. On the western edge, Sunday's El Rastro market is an absolute mob scene, but has to be experienced at least once. Then flee to one of Lavapies' cafes for some mafe (Senegalese lamb stew), tandoori, or (as always) classic taberna-style Spanish cuisine. Yum.

LA CALETA

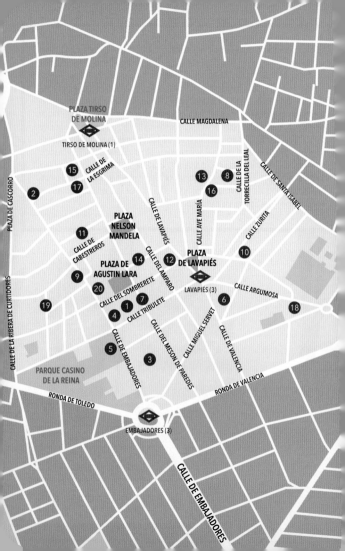

LANDMARKS

Biblioteca Escuelas Pías
Calle del Sombrerete 15
Former hermitage brilliantly transformed into a library for UNED.

El Rastro
Plaza de Cascorro
Madrid's most famous street market, every Sunday until your head explodes.

La Tabacalera
Calle de Embajadores 53
Former tobacco factory turned formal/informal artist studios & performance spaces. Funky.

Mercado San Fernando
Calle de Embajadores 41
Brilliant mercado with lots of quirk, including German beer.

Parque Casino de la Reina
Calle de Embajadores 68
Locals park with yoga, dogs, kids, and (of course) tables.

Teatro VALLE-INCLÁN
Calle de Valencia 1
Super-cool modern theater and home to the Centro Dramático Nacional.

NIGHTLIFE

7 Gau Cafe
Calle Tribulete 14
Rooftop terrace, bar, and restaurant that overlooks Lavapies from the UNED library. A must.

8 El Gato Verde
Calle de la Torrecilla del Leal 15
Lots of good beers late into the night. As it should be.

9 La Fantástica de Lavapiés
Calle de Embajadores 42
You want locals? Here they are.

10 La Huelga de Lavapiés
Calle Zurita 39
Papers and supplies for all those artists who can't afford Las Letras.

RESTAURANTS

11 Baobab
Calle de Cabestreros 1
Delicious Senegalese with outdoor seating on the plaza in front. A must.

12 Dakar Restaurant Senegalés
Calle del Amparo 61
Good local Senegalese for when Baobab doesn't have its act together.

13 Moharaj
Calle Ave María 18
Best of the Indian joints in Lavapiés, good tandoori of course.

14 El Cafelito
Calle del Sombrerete 20
The best coffee in Lavapiés, ideal for a lazy Saturday morning.

15 Taberna Antonio Sanchez
Calle del Meson de Paredes 13
Classic Spanish taberna, complete with boar's heads and wood paneling. Perfection.

16 La Caleta
Calle de los Tres Peces 21
If you like shrimp pancakes and "pescaito frito" (fried fish) like they do it in Cádiz.

SHOPPING

17 Carnicería Emilo
Calle de la Esgrima 12
Great local butcher for when you don't want to (or can't) deal with the mercado.

18 Cosmo Cash & Carry
Calle Argumosa 22
International grocery store stocking lots and lots of Indian products for home curry-cooking.

19 Galerías Piquer
Calle de la Ribera de Curtidores 29
Suite of antique stores off the eastern side of El Rastro. Slightly less mobbed.

20 Tienda Solidaria Piel de Mariposa
Calle de Embajadores
Nice little non-profit consignment shop. Treasures abound.

LA LATINA

SHOKO MADRID

EL COSACO

TEATRO LA LATINA

The final classic "old Madrid neighborhood" in our guide, La Latina doesn't disappoint. Fabulous landmarks—such as the Real Basilica de San Francisco el Grande and the giant bustling Mercado de la Cebada—are dotted throughout La Latina's narrow, picturesque streets, which are filled with cafes, shops, plazas, tourists, and plenty of Madrileños. Kids play in the plaza while their parents sip tinto de veranos under the Spanish sun and life is examined, Spanish-style (complaints about the government while eating delicious jamon de bellota...ah, Spain). We suggest following their lead and doing the same, because what is the point of working so hard that you can't enjoy life? The Western Calvinist Work Ethic is all well and good, but really, where does it get you...but we digress. It's back to working on this Not For Tourists City Guide for Madrid, and writing about the classic La Latina neighborhood.

CONTRACLUB

CALLE DE SEGOVIA

RONDA DE SEGOVIA

EL JARDÍN
DEL PRÍNCIPE
DE ANGLONA

CALLE DE
LA MORERÍA

8

7

PLAZA
GABRIEL MIRÓ

CALLE DE BAILÉN

CALLE SAN BUENAVENTURA

PLAZA DE
LA PAJA

1

PLAZA
SAN ANDRÉS

6

13

11

15

16

CALLE CAVA BAJA

LA LATINA (5)

5

PLAZA DE
LOS CARROS

PLAZA DE LA CEBADA

9

2

PLAZA PUERTA
DE MOROS

CARRERA DE
SAN FRANCISCO

4

PARQUE DE
LA CORNISA

RONDA DE SEGOVIA

10

CALLE DE TOLEDO

CALLE BASTERO

CALLE DE CARLOS ARNICHES

PLAZA GRAL.
VARA DE REY

19

20

14

17

12

1

GRAN VÍA DE SAN FRANCISCO

GLORIETA PUERTA
DE TOLEDO

3

PUERTA DE
TOLEDO (5)

PLAZA DEL
CAMPILLO DEL
NUEVO MUNDO

LA LATINA

LANDMARKS

Plaza de la Paja
Madrid as it was during the reign of the
Austrias. A hidden gem.

Mercado de la Cebada
Plaza de la Cebada
Giant (and we mean giant) mercado
that has the craziest roof ever.

Puerta de Toledo
Glorieta Puerta de Toledo
Famous portal, one of nineteen
original gates to the city.

**Real Basílica de San Francisco
el Grande**
Calle San Buenaventura 1
The granddaddy of Madrid churches.
Great back rooms, too.

Teatro La Latina
Plaza de la Cebada 2
Classic Madrid theater presenting,
well, the classics.

NIGHTLIFE

Caravan Cocktail Bar
Calle Príncipe Anglona 3
We have tried many cocktail bars in
Madrid, and we like them all.

ContraClub
Calle de Bailén 16
Rockin' (live music, DJs) club steps from
Madrid's most classic church. Of course.

Corral de la Morería Restaurant
Calle de la Moreria 17
Live flamenco and dead flesh served
in classic surroundings.

Juana La Loca
Plaza Puerta de Moros 4
Hipster Madrid pintxos bar, and
vice-versa.

Shoko Madrid
Calle de Toledo 86
Larger live music club with good
rotating mix of artists.

RESTAURANTS

11 Calle Cava Baja
--not one, but 20 restaurants all in the
narrowest street possible. Enjoy.

12 El Capricho Extremeño
Calle de Carlos Arniches 30
Always-mobbed tostas joint worth a stop,
of course.

13 El Cosaco
Plaza de la Paja 2
Russian specialties in one of our favorite
'nabes'. Nasdarovje!

14 Los Caracoles
Calle de Toledo 106
Classic Madrid bar known for its piles
and piles of snails. Yum.

15 Posada de la Villa
Calle Cava Baja 9
Amazing interior design matches classic
Spanish cuisine.

SHOPPING

16 Disfraces Paco
Calle de Toledo 52
Insane costume shop that needs to be
experienced (once).

17 El Laberinto 2
Calle de Carlos Arniches 23
Whacked-out antiques shop stuffed to
the gills with crap; awesome.

18 Fotocasion
Calle de la Ribera de Curtidores 22
Super-dangerous camera store just off
El Rastro (so don't go on Sunday).

19 La Recova
Plaza Gral. Vara de Rey 7
Modernist furniture to spend your
hard-earned dollars on.

20 Underground
Calle Bastero 16
Used clothing for the natty Madrileño
(all of them).

ARGÜELLES

CASA PACO

EL PIMIENTO VERDE

TEMPLO DE DEBOD

Surrounded on two sides by the Parque del Oeste, Argüelles has two separate personalities--first, the tourists-and-locals-laden southern end, surrounding Plaza de España, Calle Princesa, the Museo Cerralbo, Estación de Príncipe Pío (technically down the hill from the actual Argüelles neighborhood), and the Templo de Debod area of Parque del Oeste. On Argüelles's northern side, it's, well...ah...not very exciting. Which is fun too, in its way, just being able to watch some of the better-off citizens of Madrid just go about their daily business, enjoying the quieter northern section of the Parque del Oeste, and shopping at the newly-renovated Mercado Municipal De Argüelles. Right in the center of the area, inside Parque del Oeste, is the Teleférico, Madrid's not-to-be-missed aerial tram that sails over Río Manzanares and right into the heart of Madrid's Mágical sprawling park, Casa de Campo. All in all, it's not a 'nabe to be missed.

CINES PRINCESA

PARQUE DEL OESTE

AV. SÉNECA

AV. DE VALLADOLID

PASEO DE CAMOENS

PASEO DEL PINTOR ROSALES

PASEO DE MORET

MONCLOA (3)

11 6

13

CALLE DE ALTAMIRANO

17

CALLE DEL MARQUÉS DE URQUIJO

4

18

15

CALLE DE BUEN SUCESO

19

ARGÜELLES (3) (4) (6)

CALLE DE MARTÍN DE LOS HEROS

CALLE QUINTANA

12

CALLE DE LA PRINCESA

20

RÍO MANZANARES

PASEO DEL REY

PASEO DE LA FLORIDA

CALLE FERAZ

CALLE JUAN ÁLVAREZ MENDIZÁBAL

CALLE VENTURA RODRÍGUEZ

VENTURA RODRÍGUEZ (3)

5

3

7 8

1 14 16 9

PRÍNCIPE PÍO (6) (10)

10

2

CUESTA DE SAN VICENTE

PLAZA DE ESPAÑA (3) (10)

ARGÜELLES

LANDMARKS

Museo Cerralbo
Calle Ventura Rodríguez 17
Private collection of everything by the Marquis of Cerralbo. Awesome.

Plaza de España
Gathering place of all sorts of folks, with empty Edificio España looming over it all. Nice fountain.

Estación de Príncipe Pío
Paseo de la Florida 2
Huge light-filled train station/mall with in-house movie theater.

Teleférico de Madrid
Paseo del Pintor Rosales
Soar over Madrid in an aerial tram on your way to adventures in Casa de Campo.

Templo de Debod
Parque del Oeste
One of Madrid's classic attractions, with a killer overlook to boot.

NIGHTLIFE

Casa Paco
Calle Juan Álvarez Mendizábal 85
Tortillas and cervezas in a classic Madrid joint.

Cines Golem
Calle de Martín de los Heros 14
One of three great movie theaters in Plaza Princesa.

Cines Princesa
Calle de la Princesa 3
The mothership of Madrid movie theaters. 14 screens.

Cines Renoir
Calle de Martín de los Heros 12
The arthouse portion of the Renoir juggernaut.

Tablao Flamenco Las Tablas
Plaza de España 9
Classic flamenco steps from, well, everything.

RESTAURANTS

11 **Arrocería Casa de Valencia**
Paseo del Pintor Rosales 58
Paella by the park. Go for it.

12 **El Pimiento Verde**
Calle Quintana 1
Argüelles outlet of Basque goodness--monkfish, steak, artichokes all delicious.

13 **Restaurante Manolo 1934**
Calle de la Princesa 83
Oozing classic Madrid history and cuisine.

14 **Taberna La Charca**
Calle Juan Álvarez Mendizábal 7
Lovely interior, good food, perfect for post-Cerralbo analysis.

15 **Tabernícola**
Calle de Buen Suceso 20
Beautiful reboot on a fabulous corner location. Ole!

SHOPPING

16 **Fábrica de Cajas de Cartón y Sombrereras**
Calle Juan Álvarez Mendizábal 5
Because every great city needs a great hat box store.

17 **Mercado Municipal De Argüelles**
Calle de Altamirano 7
Great 2011 renovation now houses cheery local mercado.

18 **Motor Sport**
Calle del Marqués de Urquijo 43
Zoom, zoom. Motorcycles and scooters for hip Madrileños (re: all of them).

19 **Naos Libros**
Calle Quintana 12
Killer selection, especially art and architecture.

20 **Papeleria Debod**
Calle Ferraz 24
One of a hundred great Madrid stationery stores, it seems. Nice one.

CHAMBERÍ WEST

POOL AND BEER

EL TENDIDO

FARO DE MONCLOA

OK, now we're starting to get into the neighborhoods where everyone actually lives. Yes, center Madrid is fabulous, but you'll pay for it, in more ways than one--for instance, the constant crush of tourists to complement your high rent and ancient plumbing. Enter: Chamberí. One of those unusual cartographic neighborhoods in that it's wider east-west than north-south, Chamberí sprawls out just north of the center and is bisected by Calle de Bravo Murillo. It's nothing fancy--just great shops, food, and culture, all without any kind of need to cater to the world's twentysomethings blanketing Madrid for their Hen Parties (shudder!) and Spring Breaks. So our advice is to simply walk the streets and take time to poke your head into the Parroquia de San Cristóbal and San Rafael, catch a film festival at Sala Berlanger, and stop by for some salmorejo and a cerveza at El Tendido; life, in Chamberí.

SALA BERLANGA

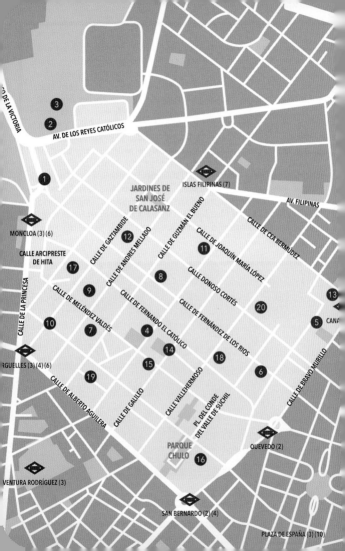

JARDINES DE
SAN JOSÉ
DE CALASANZ

ISLAS FILIPINAS (7)

AV. FILIPINAS

AV. DE LOS REYES CATÓLICOS

DE LA VICTORIA

MONCLOA (3) (6)

CALLE ARCIPRESTE
DE HITA

CALLE DE CEA BERMÚDEZ

CALLE DE GAZTAMBIDE

CALLE DE GUZMÁN EL BUENO

CALLE DE JOAQUÍN MARÍA LÓPEZ

CALLE DE ANDRÉS MELLADO

CALLE DONOSO CORTÉS

CALLE DE LA PRINCESA

CALLE DE MELÉNDEZ VALDÉS

CALLE DE FERNANDO EL CATÓLICO

CALLE DE FERNÁNDEZ DE LOS RÍOS

CANA

RGUELLES (3) (4) (6)

CALLE DE ALBERTO AGUILERA

CALLE DE GALILEO

CALLE VALLEHERMOSO

CALLE DE BRAVO MURILLO

PL. DEL CONDE
DEL VALLE DE SUCHIL

QUEVEDO (2)

VENTURA RODRÍGUEZ (3)

PARQUE
CHULO

SAN BERNARDO (2) (4)

PLAZA DE ESPAÑA (3) (10)

LANDMARKS

Arco de la Victoria
Av. Arco de la Victoria
We won! We won! Whatever it was…

Faro de Moncloa
Av. Arco de la Victoria 2
Cool observation deck but the
Teleférico is cooler.

Museo de América
Av. de los Reyes Católicos 6
We came, we saw, we conquered…

**Parroquia del Santísimo Cristo
de la Victoria**
Calle de Fernando el Católico 45
With a name this long, it's got to be
important.

**Parroquia de San Cristobal
and San Rafael**
Calle de Bravo Murillo 39
See above.

RESTAURANTS

Restaurant El Llar
Calle de Fernández de los
Asturian goodness in a nice space.

El Tendido
Calle de Andres Mellado 20
An absolute Madrid classic.

Membibre
Calle de Guzmán el Bueno 40
Delicious corner spot with a few
(of course) outdoor tables.

Nakeima
Calle de Meléndez Valdés 54
Crazy-assed, crazy-busy dumpling
and tapas spot. Good luck.

Restaurant Tres Bocas
Calle de Gaztambide 11
A bit of everything, just like Madrid.
Nice.

NIGHTLIFE

Pool and Beer
Calle de Joaquín María López 17
We are completely in agreement with
the ethos of this establishment.

Sala Berlanga
Calle de Andres Mellado 53
Movie house with film festivals and more.

Teatros de Canal
Calle de Cea Bermúdez 1
One of the centers of the Madrid
performing arts scene.

Teatro Galileo
Calle de Galileo 39
Theater for all, music for some.

SHOPPING

Esmalper
Calle de Galileo 27
Toys and figurines for everyone who's
into toys and figurines.

Marcial Pons Librero
Pl. del Conde del Valle de Súchil 8
Nice bookshop on the plaza.

Mercado de Moncloa
Calle Vallehermoso 36
Just another perfect Madrid mercado.

Mercado Vallehermoso
Calle Vallehermoso 36
See above.

Salvador Bachiller
Calle de Alberto Aguilera 54
Bags and luggage for the hip set.

Tienda Tintín
Calle Donoso Cortés 20
Yes, a Tintín store. Yes, it's cool.

CHAMBERÍ EAST

BAR MÉNTRIDA

NEW YORK BURGER

MUSEO SOROLLA ◎

This is our favorite part of Chamberí, since it has the awesome Chamberí Mercado, the Museo Sorolla, as well as our favorite outdoor plaza in all of Madrid, the perfectly symmetrical and circular Plaza de Olavide. Calle de Trafalgar goes underground the plaza, and all other roads into it dead-end or bend backwards away from it. It's a lovely oasis, as is Chamberí's eastern edge--the tree-and-embassy-lined Paseo de la Castellana. There are lots of government offices, schools, and other official-looking structures here, some with interior walled-off gardens you can't get to, but in the end, though, just like Chamberí's western half, most of this 'nabe is about regular life for regular folks, and we couldn't love it more. Grab a delicious burger at Burger Joint, New York Burger, or Mentidero de la Villa, watch the world pass by at Whitby, and finish up with some dessert at the Chocolat Factory. Finis.

BAR MÉNTRIDA 🍸

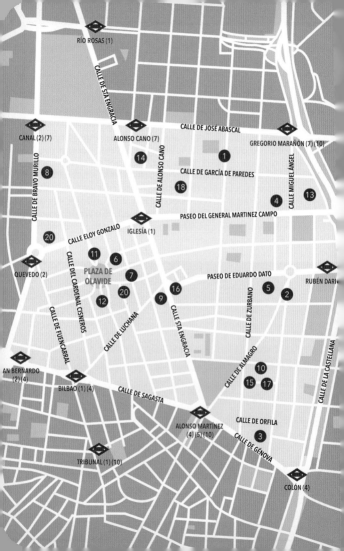

RÍO ROSAS (1)

CALLE DE STA ENGRACIA

CALLE DE JOSÉ ABASCAL

CANAL (2) (7)

ALONSO CANO (7)

GREGORIO MARAÑÓN (7) (10)

CALLE DE ALONSO CANO

CALLE MIGUEL ÁNGEL

14

CALLE DE BRAVO MURILLO

8

1

CALLE DE GARCÍA DE PAREDES

18

4

13

PASEO DEL GENERAL MARTÍNEZ CAMPO

20

CALLE ELOY GONZALO

IGLESIA (1)

QUEVEDO (2)

CALLE DEL CARDENAL CISNEROS

11

6

PLAZA DE OLAVIDE

7

PASEO DE EDUARDO DATO

RUBÉN DARÍ

20

16

5

2

12

9

CALLE DE ZURBANO

CALLE DE FUENCARRAL

CALLE DE LUCHANA

CALLE STA ENGRACIA

CALLE DE ALMAGRO

CALLE DE LA CASTELLANA

AN BERNARDO (2) (4)

10

BILBAO (1) (4)

CALLE DE SAGASTA

15

17

CALLE DE ORFILA

ALONSO MARTÍNEZ (4) (5) (10)

CALLE DE GÉNOVA

3

TRIBUNAL (1) (10)

COLÓN (4)

CHAMBERÍ - EAST

LANDMARKS

Basilica Parroquia La Milagrosa
Calle de García de Paredes 45
Just another amazing Spanish church.

Colegio de Ingenieros de Caminos, Canales y Puertos
Calle de Almagro 42
One of the most beautiful buildings in Madrid.

Galería Marlborough
Calle de Orfila 5
Great, modern gallery--always something to argue over, at least.

Museo Sorolla
Paseo del General Martínez Campos 37
Pay homage to the master; nice back garden.

Parroquia San Fermín de los Navarros
Paseo de Eduardo Dato 10
A bit brutalist on the outside, more than beautiful inside.

Plaza de Olavide
One of the most perfectly-designed public spaces on Planet Earth. Promise.

NIGHTLIFE

7 Bar Méntrida
Plaza de Olavide 3
One of several options for drinks on the plaza.

8 Cines Verdi
Calle Bravo Murillo 28
One of the few cinemas in Madrid that screens movies in their original version.

9 Teatros Luchana
Calle de Luchana 38
A mix of family and adult theater, some concerts.

10 Whitby
Calle de Almagro 22
We don't know why we like to drink here, we just do. And we do.

RESTAURANTS

11 Burger Joint
Calle Eloy Gonzalo 12
And what a joint. Recommended.

12 Mandralisca
Calle del Cardenal Cisneros 39
One of our favorite tapas in Chamberí.

13 New York Burger
Calle Miguel Ángel 16
Maybe not New York, but at least authentically American.

14 Premiata Forneria Ballaro
Calle de Sta Engracia 90
Utterly stylish Italian with wood oven for 'za.

15 Restaurante El Mentidero de la Villa
Calle de Almagro 20
Two spaces, stylish, we just like it.

SHOPPING

16 Carnicería Ismael
Calle de Sta Engracia 39
If you can't find what you need at the mercado, there is always Ismael.

17 Crustó Bakery Zurbano
Calle de Zurbano 26
Fabulous bakery, lovely space. Enjoy.

18 Mercado de Chamberí
Calle de Alonso Cano 10
One of the grandmasters of Madrid Mercados.

19 Pastafresca
Glorieta de Quevedo 7
Super-small fresh pasta shop on Quevedo; nice one.

20 Vino & Compañía
Plaza de Olavide 5
Pretty wine shop on Plaza Olavide; take a peek.

SALAMANCA

TATEL MADRID 🍸

CAZORLA 🍴

MUSEO DE ARTE PÚBLICO

Welcome to Fancy Madrid. Everything is clean and perfect in this neighborhood, one of Madrid's classiest shopping areas (the area around Calle Serrano and Calle Ayala is called the Golden Mile). That doesn't mean it's boring, or that there's nothing to see however. Salamanca has culture oozing from its pores, from the art and performances on tap at Fundación Juan March, to the amazing collection of art and artifacts at Museo Lázaro Galdiano, to the brilliance of the Museo Arqueológico Nacional, where you can get lost for hours, pouring over Roman legal tablets and Visigothic coins. Don't miss the outdoor sculpture at Museo de Arte Público, either, while strolling Paseo de la Castellana. The food (especially at Street XO and Cascabel) is delicious, the mercados are amazing (Platea may be the poshest mercado in Europe), and the drinks, as always, are stiff, from the fancy smoking cocktails at TATEL to the dive-bar ethos at Cofradía. And Mantequerias Bravos may be our favorite gourmet market anywhere.

COFRADÍA M.A.D 🍸

SALAMANCA

LANDMARKS

Fundación Juan March
Calle de Castelló 77
All brilliant here--exhibits, shop, garden, performance spaces.

Museo Arqueológico Nacional
Calle de Serrano 13
Possibly one of the best archeology museums in the world. Awesome.

Museo de Arte Público
Paseo de la Castellana 40
Outdoor sculpture park under a bridge. Sublime.

Museo Lázaro Galdiano,
Calle de Serrano 122
Very old books. We mean VERY old books. And a Bosch. Crazy.

Parroquia de San Manuel y San Benito
Calle de Alcalá 83
Giant church across the street from Retiro Park. Stunning mosaics.

NIGHTLIFE

Arts Club Madrid
Calle de Velázquez 96
Hipper than thou, but go once anyway. Also plenty of food (it's Madrid, after all).

Gabana Club
Calle de Velázquez 6
THE posh nightclub in Madrid.

Cofradía M.A.D
Calle de Juan Bravo 57
A dive bar in a rich neighborhood! We're MAD for it.

The Geographic Club
Calle de Alcalá 141
Sip cocktails and feel like an explorer while surrounded by objects from all over the world.

TATEL Madrid
Paseo de la Castellana 36
Uber-hip joint owned by athletes serving cocktails that smoke and stuff like that. Go once. But go.

RESTAURANTS

11 Cascabel
El Corte Inglés, Calle de Serrano 52
Skip the lines at StreetXo and eat some of Madrid's best Mexican. Underrated by a mile.

12 Casa Carola
Calle de Padilla 54
Classic Salamanca joint which you'll realize the second you walk in.

13 Cazorla
Calle de Castello 99
Classic Madrid restaurant with service to match. Just about perfect.

14 Lateral Castellana 42
Paseo de la Castellana 42
Our favorite Lateral; tons of outdoor seating, love the design.

15 StreetXo
El Corte Inglés, Calle de Serrano 52
Loud, brash, crazy fusion from Munoz. Worth the line once, at least.

SHOPPING

16 Delirium Books
Calle de Ayala 10
Will cause tremors; rare books always do that to us.

17 Juana Limón
Calle de O'Donnell 15
Friendly juices and pastries from Spanish master Joaquín de Alba.

18 Mantequerías Bravo
Calle de Ayala 24
Absolutely bang-on French/Spanish gourmet food/wine shop. Brilliant.

19 Mercado de la Paz
Calle de Ayala 28
Great mercado with lots and lots of places to buy foie gras (it's Salamanca, after all…).

20 Platea Madrid
Calle de Goya 5-7
Unbelievably posh mercado with gorgeous interior spaces. Nothing else like it anywhere.

EL RETIRO / IBIZA

BAR MARTÍN

TABERNA ARZÁBAL

MUSEO DEL PRADO

Landmark central. Art? How about spending a week or so exploring all that the Prado, Spain's most famous museum, has to offer? Architecture? Gaze in wonder at the sprawling Madrid City Hall, the Ayuntamiento de Madrid. Nature? Between the Real Jardín Botánico and Retiro Park itself, you can spend a year cataloguing all the trees, plants, flowers, gardens, and fountains that you see. When you're done with all that, don't forget the amazing models at the Museo Naval and the classic telescopes at the Observatorio Astronómico de Madrid. Tired yet? No worries, plenty of benches and lawns at Retiro to soak up the Spanish sun before dipping your toe into Ibiza's neighborhood-y tapas bars and restaurants. It's a welcome respite from the massed tourists along the (otherwise gorgeous) Paseo del Prado and long lines of the Prado itself. Our advice: become a member. It's worth it.

HOTEL RITZ TERRACE

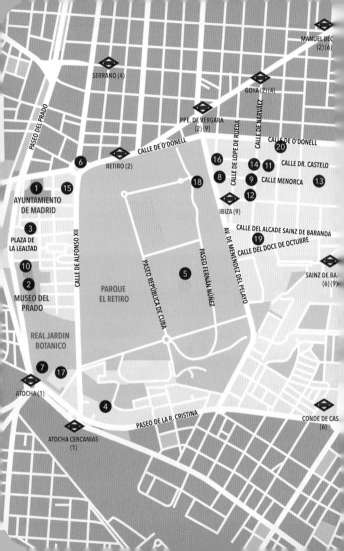

EL RETIRO / IBIZA

LANDMARKS

Ayuntamiento de Madrid
Plaza Cibeles 1A
Madrid's unbelievably ornate city hall, with an observatory at the top.

Museo Nacional del Prado
Paseo del Prado
The mothership. All the guys are here--Goya, Velázquez, El Bosco, Ribera... those guys.

Museo Naval
Paseo del Prado 5
Awesome Naval museum with amazing models and generally cool exhibits.

Observatorio Astronómico de Madrid
Calle de Alfonso XII
You won't see much of the stars, but the telescopes are neat.

Palacio de Cristal
Paseo República de Cuba 4
One of Retiro's most famous sights; the art inside is curated by the Reina.

Puerta de Alcalá
Famed in story and song, but not all that impressive.

Real Jardín Botánico
Plaza de Murillo 2
Stunning (though not free) botanic garden steps from the Prado and Retiro.

NIGHTLIFE

8 Bar Martín
Av. de Menéndez Pelayo 17
Classic Madrid watering hole across the street from Retiro.

9 Cine Renoir Retiro
Calle de Narváez 42
Fresh flicks from the Renoir folks. Fabulous.

10 Hotel Ritz Terrace
Plaza de la Lealtad 5
Well, of course. Gin tonic, por favor.

RESTAURANTS

11 La Castela
Calle Dr. Castelo 22
Classy reboot of old Madrid taberna. Nice one.

12 La Catapa
Calle Menorca 14
Perfect tapas and wines by the glass a block from Retiro; we love it.

13 La Hoja
Calle Dr. Castelo 48
Awesome Asturian palace of deliciousness; love the interior.

14 La Montería
Calle de Lope de Rueda 35
Both classic and postmodern tapas. Inventive.

15 Restaurante Vinoteca García de la Navarra
Calle de Montalbán 3
Fancy Spanish food & wine for a fancy night.

16 Taberna Arzábal
Calle Menéndez Pelayo 13
An elegant tavern with a great variety of wine.

SHOPPING

17 Cuesta de Moyano Bookstalls
Calle Claudio Moyano
Brilliant bookstalls lining the southern part of Retiro; great finds always!

18 Feria del Libro
Paseo Fernán Núñez, Retiro Park
Retiro's giant annual book fair is here; totally amazing and absorbing.

19 Pzes
Calle del Doce de Octubre 11
Aquarium; hey, we're all just little fish swimming in the wide open sea.

20 Tea Shop Narváez
Calle de Narváez 31
Cutest little tea shop this side of Retiro.

RÍOS ROSAS

CERVECERÍA EL DOBLE

CASA FONZO

NUEVOS MINISTERIOS

We just love this area. Known for its perfect storm of delicious restaurants, especially along the Calle de Ponzano, Ríos Rosas has two of Madrid's greatest interior spaces--the main room at the Museo Geominero, and the exhibition space at the Sala Canal de Isabel II. The former's Victorian-era style of a giant cabinet of curiosities, coupled with a stunning stained-glass ceiling, is only rivaled by Canal Isabel's circular, industrialized aesthetic of a former water management plant turned into a deliciously-curated postmodern art exhibition space. In between these two can't-miss spaces are dozens of great restaurants and bars along the Calle de Ponzano and surrounding streets; eat your way from Le Qualitè Tasca to Taberna AliPío Ramos, with a nightcap at La Máquina Chamberí or La Parroquia de Pablo. At some point, Le Poncelet Cheese Bar is also a must. Then it's time to hit the gym, or just pass out.

LA MÁQUINA CHAMBERÍ

RÍOS ROSAS

LANDMARKS

Hospital de Jornaleros de Maudes
Calle de Maudes 17
Yes, it really is a hospital.
Weird but pretty.

Museo Geominero
Calle de Ríos Rosas 23
Cool geological museum with an
absolutely stunning interior.

Nuevos Ministerios
Paseo de la Castellana
Hulking, sprawling government complex
everyone tries to avoid.

Sala Canal de Isabel II
Calle Santa Engracia 125
Old circular water plant now converted
into brilliant art exhibition space.

Santa Maria del Silencio
*Calle de Raimundo Fernández
Villaverde 18A*
Sssshhh...quiet

NIGHTLIFE

Cervecería El Doble
Calle de Ponzano 17
Because two beers are better than
one, silly, of course.

Cine Conde Duque Santa Engracia
Calle Santa Engracia 132
Catch a flick and then go eat on Calle
de Ponzano.

La Máquina Chamberí
Calle de Ponzano 39
This is a perfect machine; bar in front,
restaurant in back.

La Parroquia de Pablo
Calle de Breton de los Herreros 16
Because everyone should have their
own church, including Pablo.

Santa Teresa Shop
Calle de Ponzano 93
Gazpacho cocktails? Why not?

RESTAURANTS

11 **Atelier Belge Restaurante**
Calle de Breton de los Herreros 39
Hip Belgian joint if you need a break
from Spanish classics.

12 **Casa Fonzo**
Calle de Ponzano 60
Argentinean cuisine. Empanadas a
must (of course).

13 **Le Qualitè Tasca**
Calle de Ponzano 48
Spanish... with a bit of fusion

14 **Picsa**
Calle de Ponzano 76
Because who doesn't like
Argentinian pizza?

15 **Sylkar**
Calle de Espronceda 17
Possibly the best tortilla de patatas in
Madrid. And the best torrijas.

16 **Taberna AliPío Ramos**
Calle de Ponzano 30
Hundred-year-old taberna anchoring the
gastronomic perfection of Calle
de Ponzano.

17 **Toque de Sal**
Calle de Ponzano 46
A touch of salt makes everything better, as
this fancy Mediterranean bistro will tell you.

SHOPPING

18 **Mercato Italiano**
Calle de Ríos Rosas 50
Cute Italian shop/cafe with delicious
focaccia, of course.

19 **Pastelería La Maravilla**
Calle de Ríos Rosas 41
Not just a pastelería, but also a
croissantería!

20 **Poncelet Cheese Bar**
Calle de José Abascal 61
The Poncelet cheese masters have added
what was missing to cheese: a bar.

CUATRO CAMINOS

LATERAL

TABERNA ARZÁBAL

TORRE PICASSO

We're not exactly sure which four roads they're talking about here, but it doesn't really matter. It is what it is: a neighborhood with a split personality. The eastern half, filled with malls, big box stores, chain restaurants, and skyscrapers, and the western half, filled with, well...perfection, in the form of a nice sleepy little Madrid neighborhood. We guess it's a metaphor for any city; you're gonna need huge government buildings filled with grubby little clerks pushing paper, skyscrapers filled with international bankers doing the dirty work of making sure the rich, under no circumstances, pay their fair share, and shopping malls catering to those same rich tourists' need to prove their wealth by buying $2,000 bags and $1,500 shoes. You'll see us instead at Mercado de Maravillas shopping for cheese, browsing artist's books with the staff at Ivorypress, and having a drink at El Quinto Vino.

DISCOTECA TARTUFO

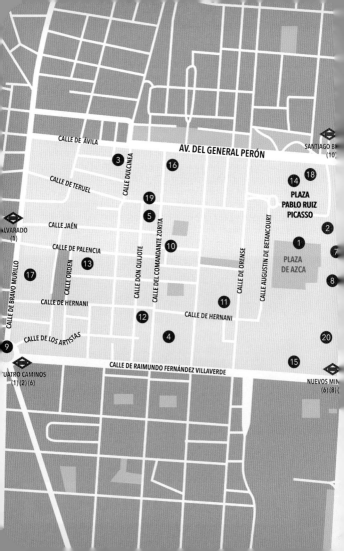

CUATRO CAMINOS

LANDMARKS

Plaza de Azca
Paseo de la Castellana
Decent enough outdoor space, sometimes (thankfully) filled with food trucks.

Parroquia San Antonio de Cuatro Caminos
Calle de Bravo Murillo 150
Yet another Spanish church, this one dedicated to Saint Anthony.

Torre Picasso
Plaza Pablo Ruiz Picasso
One of Madrid's skyscrapers. Skip it, get some tapas instead.

RESTAURANTS

Arroceria Bahía
Calle Dulcinea 65
You should know by now that this means paella. Yum.

Asador Guetaria
Calle del Comandante Zorita 8
Classic Basque joint serving up deliciousness, as always.

Goizeko Kabi
Calle del Comandante Zorita 37
Posh dining but totally delicious.

Lateral
Paseo de la Castellana 89
The furthest north this chain has made it so far; keep going, guys!

La Vaca Argentina
Paseo de la Castellana 87
Dependable-enough steakhouse, gracias Argentina.

Marisquería Norte Sur
Calle de Bravo Murillo 97
Delicious seafood, whichever direction you choose to come from.

Taberna Gaztelupe
Calle del Comandante Zorita 32
The old-world half of the Gaztelupe empire.

NIGHTLIFE

11 Discoteca Tartufo
Calle de Hernani 75
If you must dance in this neighborhood, this is the place.

12 El Quinto Vino
Calle de Hernani 48
A classic Madrileña tavern. Check out the pictures on the walls.

SHOPPING

13 Bicimanía
Calle de Palencia 20
We're crazy for bikes, and so are the Spaniards.

14 Chocolate Factory
Av. del General Perón 40
The only kind of factory we'd ever want to work in.

15 El Corte Inglés
Calle de Raimundo Fernández Villaverde 79
In case the one near you isn't enough, here's another.

16 Ivorypress
Calle del Comandante Zorita 46
Brilliant artist-centered bookshop and gallery; sublime.

17 Mercado de Maravillas
Calle de Bravo Murillo 122
Just another bustling Madrid mercado to love and cherish.

18 Moda Shopping
Av. del General Perón 38
Giant indoor mall with glass ceiling. Your choice.

19 Pastelería Mallorca
Calle del Comandante Zorita 39
Perfect pastries for the perfectly dressed.

20 Zara
Paseo de la Castellana 79
The empire comes to Cuatro Caminos; destroys all pretenders.

EL VISO / CASTELLANA

TABERNA CAZORLA

CAFÉ SAIGÓN

AUDITORIO NACIONAL

Welcome to El Viso, home to the rich and famous of Spain (well, Madrid anyway). Here you can find the mansions of Spanish politicians, celebrities and athletes, as well as Restaurante Zalacaín, one of the Madrid's poshest. But don't let this fool you; there's still plenty to do even though rich neighborhoods are generally boring. If you're in the mood for culture, you can pay a visit to the spectacular National Science Museum or enjoy a classical musical evening at AuditoRío Nacional de Música. If you're more into pub crawls, you're in luck: this area has some of the best football bars to grab a bite before the match (for those of you non-sports types: Spanish soccer legends Real Madrid's home games are played just across the street from this neighborhood in Estadio Santiago Bernabéu) and celebrate or drown your sorrows afterwards. In the end, there IS something for everyone.

EL VISO/CASTELLANA

LANDMARKS

Auditorio Nacional de Música
Calle del Príncipe de Vergara 146
Madrid's main concert hall for classical music.

Museo Nacional de Ciencias Naturales
Calle de José Gutiérrez Abascal 2
Giant, sprawling, amazing.

Plaza de la República Argentina
The dolphins in the fountain are pretty cute, we think.

RESTAURANTS

Café Saigón
Calle de María de Molina 4
Decent Vietnamese bound to slake hunger after the Natural Sciences museum.

Fass
Calle Rodríguez Marín 84
German all the way, from brats to wurst; also a German products shop.

Hikari Sushi Bar
Paseo de la Castellana 57
Posh sushi bar inside Hotel Hesperia; good for (light) business lunches.

La Ancha
Calle del Príncipe de Vergara 204
Classic Madrid; go for the Armando steak.

Mayte Commodore
Pl. de la República Argentina 5
Madrid's hot spot in the 60s.
Ava Gardner was here.

Restaurante Zalacaín
Calle Álvarez de Baena 4
Posh, exclusive...did we say posh, exclusive?

VIPS Velázquez
Calle de Velázquez 136
Schizophrenic Spanish diner/shop chain that has to be experienced at least once.

NIGHTLIFE

11 Casa Puebla
Calle Gutiérrez Solana 4
Perfect pre- or post-match tapas and cervezas near Bernabéu.

12 El Refugio
Calle San Juan de la Salle 6
For those about to rock.

13 Fiat Café
Calle de Serrano 197
A fancier bar to watch the match or to listen to some live music.

14 La Daniela
Calle Gutiérrez Solana 2
Another classic spot to watch El Clasico.

15 Restaurante/Taberna Cazorla
Calle Rodríguez Marín 80
One of the best Andalusian places in Madrid.

16 Si Señor
Paseo de la Castellana 128
Margaritas and other less important things on Castellana. Enjoy.

SHOPPING

17 El Miajon De Los Castuos
Paseo de la Habana 19
Pata de jamón, cheese, wine… what else do you need?

18 Heladería La Romana
Paseo de la Habana 27
Because even the Spanish scream for ice cream.

19 Retrocycle
Av. Dr. Arce 32
Perfect bike shop with all the accessories.

CHAMARTÍN

EL ENFRIADOR

RESTAURANTE SACHA

SANTIAGO BERNABÉU

One piece of advice: don't go into this neighborhood on El Clasico nights. Or do, if you want to get trampled to death by a mass of football fans who have come from all over the world to see Real Madrid and Barcelona play. That's right, we're in Chamartín, home of the Bernabéu and for many Spaniards, Madrid's most important spot. Have a walk around the stadium and pay an exorbitant price to access the Bernabéu Museum, where you can admire Real Madrid's eleven European Cups- even if you're not a football fan, you have to admit that eleven European Cups is pretty impressive. But don't worry, not everything in this neighborhood revolves about football. You can also do some shopping at Madrid's fanciest supermarket chain, go to yet another mercado, or talk about the match in one of the neighborhood's bars. OK, we were kidding: everything revolves around football.

BOOM ROOM

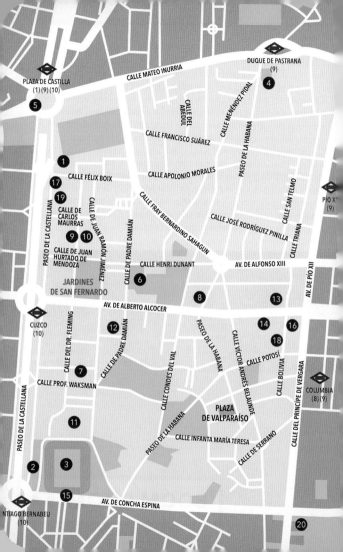

CHAMARTÍN

LANDMARKS

Centro de Exposiciones Arte Canal
Paseo de la Castellana 214
Former canal management space turned
into rotating art exhibitions; nice one.

Bernabéu Tour
Paseo de la Castellana 142
Live the dream.

Estadio Santiago Bernabéu
Paseo de la Castellana 142
The mothership of Spanish soccer.
Ugly outside, magic inside.

Palacete de los Duques de Pastrana
Paseo de la Habana 208
Dead duke's digs; now an event space.

Plaza Castilla
Weird-ass sculpture from Calatrava
You can't win them all.

RESTAURANTS

El Telégrafo
Calle de Padre Damián 44
Great seafooder with awesome decor
and (of course) outdoor space.

Omar Restaurante
Calle Prof. Waksman 11
Friendly, delicious authentic Turkish.
Enjoy.

Restaurante Juanita Cruz
Paseo de la Habana 105
Cool, hip space; we're a bit torn on
the food, but try it.

Restaurante Rubaiyat
Calle de Juan Ramón Jiménez 37
Sprawling sizzling delicious Brazilian
with fabulous outdoor spaces.

Restaurante Sacha
Calle de Juan Hurtado de Mendoza 11
Alternative bistro, impossible to get in
without a reservation.

NIGHTLIFE

Bar La Huella
Calle del Dr. Fleming 4
Next to Bernabéu, perfect place to grab
some tapas before the match.

Boom Room (Antigua sala Marmara)
Calle de Padre Damián 23
Nightclub beneath a hotel, only go if
you're forty (gasp!).

El Enfriador
Av. de Alberto de Alcocer 47
Be prepared to talk about football.

La Cocina Rock Bar
Av. de Alberto de Alcocer 48
Live music bar; you might also catch a
karaoke night.

Realcafé Bernabéu
Puerta 30 Estadio Santiago Bernabéu
Expensive, but you get to see the Bern-
abéu field while you eat!

Taj Mahal
Calle Bolivia 28
Cocktails and shisha, the perfect
way to relax.

SHOPPING

Castellana 200 - Paseo Comercial
Paseo de la Castellana 196
Huge shopping complex, you'll get lost
for hours.

Mercado de Chamartín
Calle Bolivia 9
Go-to mercado for everyone who lives
in northeast Madrid. Great selection of
everything.

Supermercados Sánchez Romero
Calle de Carlos Maurras 2
Madrid's fanciest supermarket chain.
It even has a terrace.

SOLO de UVA
Calle del Príncipe de Vergara 210
Just lots and lots of wine.

TETUÁN

THE IRISH ROVER 🍸

OCAFÚ 🍴

PALACIO DE CONGRESOS ◉

Tetuán is definitely a neighborhood of contrasts. On the right, you can find La Castellana--men in suits rushing to work past fancy seafood restaurants such as Restaurante L'Albufera and Marisquería La Chalana. On the left--one of Madrid's most diverse neighborhoods, much to your surprise. Take a walk around Calle Bravo Murillo, where reggaeton plays while you're smelling the delicious food coming from Latin American joints such as Restaurante Reina del Quinche and La Papita Criolla. When the sun sets down, move to the other side of the neighborhood and grab dinner and drinks at the Irish Rover, an incredibly cute pub that's at least trying to be Irish (with an outdoor terrace, of course). Afterwards, the options are limitless; keep drinking at the neighborhood's bars, listen to some flamenco at Teatro Gran Maestre or feel like a sailor at Moby Dick. Whatever you feel like.

LAS JARRITAS

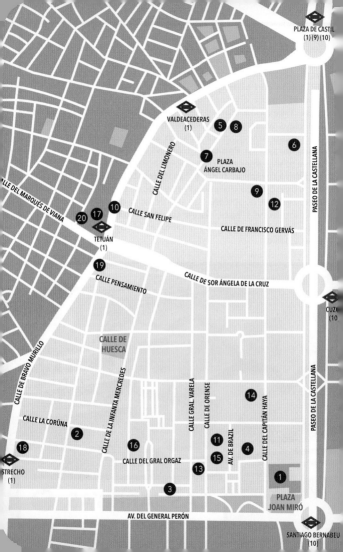

PLAZA DE CASTIL
(1) (9) (10)

VALDEACEDERAS
(1)

PLAZA
ÁNGEL CARBAJO

CALLE DEL LIMONERO

CALLE DEL MARQUÉS DE VIANA

CALLE SAN FELIPE

CALLE DE FRANCISCO GERVÁS

PASEO DE LA CASTELLANA

TETUÁN
(1)

CALLE PENSAMIENTO

CALLE DE SOR ÁNGELA DE LA CRUZ

CUZ
(10

CALLE DE
HUESCA

CALLE DE BRAVO MURILLO

CALLE GRAL. VARELA

CALLE DE ORENSE

CALLE DEL CAPITÁN HAYA

PASEO DE LA CASTELLANA

CALLE LA CORÚNA

CALLE DE LA INFANTA MERCEDES

AV. DE BRAZIL

CALLE DEL GRAL ORGAZ

STRECHO
(1)

PLAZA
JOAN MIRÓ

AV. DEL GENERAL PERÓN

SANTIAGO BERNABEU
(10)

LANDMARKS

1 Palacio de Congresos de Madrid
Paseo de la Castellana 99
Giant exposition hall for, well, giant expositions.

2 Museo Tiflológico (ONCE)
Calle la Coruña 18
Art, sculpture, and materials museum dedicated to the blind; very cool.

RESTAURANTS

3 Kabuki
Av. Presidente Carmona 2
Japanese Mediterranean fusion. Delicious.

4 Kilómetros de Pizza
Av. de Brasil 6
They're not kidding. Quite good, nice outdoor options too.

5 Los Arroces de Segis
Calle de la Infanta Mercedes 109
Perfect paella for patrons of all places.

6 Marisquería La Chalana
Paseo de la Castellana 179
Seafooder with large selection of (different) grilled whole fish. Nice one.

7 Mesón Txistu
Plaza Ángel Carbajo 6
Chuletóns, solomillos, entrecotes, tartars--meat any way you like it.

8 Ocafú
Calle de la Infanta Mercedes 98
Try the tortilla de Betanzos. You won't regret it.

9 Restaurante L'Albufera
Calle del Capitán Haya 43
Fancy paellas in the fancy inside terrace of a hotel.

10 Restaurante Reina del Quinche
Calle Tablada 6
Small Ecuadorian place, cheap and authentic.

NIGHTLIFE

11 The Irish Rover
Calle del Dr. Fleming 4
Sumptuously-decorated bar, great gin tonics.

12 Klimt
Calle del Capitán Haya 48
Sumptuously-decorated bar, great gin tonics.

13 Las Jarritas
Calle de Orense 39
Because every neighborhood needs (one) sports bar.

14 La Taberna de Emyfa
Calle del Capitán Haya 11
Every neighborhood needs a second sports bar.

15 Moby Dick
Av. de Brasil 5
Great music venue with awesome decor.

16 Teatro Gran Maestre
Calle del Gral Orgaz 17
Grand theater, check out its f lamenco nights

SHOPPING

17 Cafetería NEBRASKA
Calle de Bravo Murillo 291
It used to be a classic Spanish chain but there is only one left now.

18 La Antigua Churrería
Calle de Bravo Murillo 190
Founded in 1913; the churros are still great.

19 La Papita CRíolla
Calle Pensamiento 1
Colombian coffee place, try the bananas on toast.

20 Mercado Municipal De Tetuán
Calle del Marqués de Víana 4
Biggest, best mercado in Tetuán. Always a pleasure.

VICENTE CALDERÓN

SAL DE HIELO

EL RANCHO MADRID

RÍO MANZANARES

Welcome to the south of Madrid, home to Río Manzanares and what used to be the iconic stadium Vicente Calderón. For many Madrileños it's not worth going this far- especially now that Atlético de Madrid, the city's other team, has abandoned its old stadium for a new shiny one in the north of Madrid- but don't listen to them, there's still plenty of things to do here. For starters, check out Río Manzanares, Madrid's small river, and the beautiful bridges that surround it: Puente de Toledo, Puente de Andorra and Puente de Segovia. There's also some awesome views of the historic centre of Madrid. We recommend having lunch at La Fogata, a delicious Colombian restaurant with a good view of Palacio Real. If you're feeling thirsty, why not grab a drink at Terraza Atenas, a lovely outdoors terrace with great mojitos and gin tonics. And if you're feeling racy, one of Madrid's two kart tracks is just around the corner.

PARQUE DE SAN ISIDRO

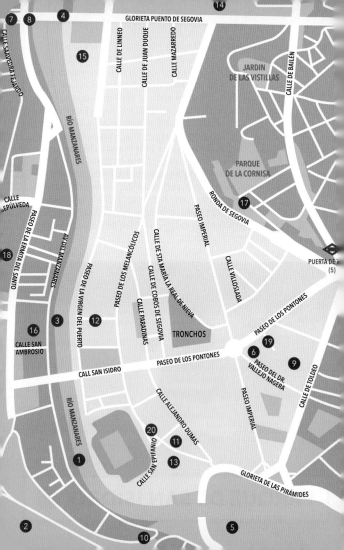

VICENTE CALDERÓN

LANDMARKS

Río Manzanares
It's tiny, but it's the city's only river.
What can you do.

Parque de San Isidro
Great park on the other side of the river,
check out the ermita (hermitage) in
honour of the saint.

Puente de Andorra
Cool three-pronged footbridge over
the mighty Manzanares.

Puente de Segovia
Madrid's oldest bridge, if you're into
bridges. Which you should be.

Puente de Toledo
300-year-old baroque bridge by
Pedro de Ribera. Check it out.

RESTAURANTS

Arrocería Imperial
Paseo del Dr. Vallejo Nagera 54
Because every neighborhood
needs a paella place.

Chacón
Calle Saavedra Fajardo 16
Octopus and beer from Galicia
(where else?).

Colombiano La Fogata
Glorieta Puente de Segovia 1
Great Colombian with awesome views
to Puente de Segovia and Palacio Real.

Sal de Hielo
Calle Toledo 140
New hip restaurant with a good
selection of Spanish food.

Mesón A Ría de Noia
Paseo de Extremadura 1
Small and rustic, try the pimientos
de padrón.

NIGHTLIFE

11 **El Rancho Madrid**
Paseo de los Melancólicos 77
Tango nights and Argentinian meat,
and vice versa.

12 **Mesón San Isidro**
Paseo del Quince de Mayo 15
Bar and tapas in honour of the saint.

13 **El Chiscón de la Ribera**
Calle San Epifanio 7
Neighborhood bar, we like the ball
pool for kids.

14 **Terraza Atenas**
Parque de Atenas
Awesome mojitos in a lovely
outdoors terrace.

15 **Sala Riviera**
Paseo Bajo de la Virgen del Puerto
One of Madrid's classic concert venues.

16 **Sala Trivial**
Calle San Ambrosio 8
Liberal club, for the more open minded…

17 **Teseo Teatro**
Ronda de Segovia 61
Theater nights happen here.

SHOPPING

18 **Carlos Sainz Center**
Calle Sepúlveda 3
One of Madrid's two Kart tracks is in
this neighborhood. Run like the wind!

19 **ElectricBricks**
Paseo de los Pontones 23
LEGO shop; do we need to say more?

20 **Tienda Oficial Atlético de Madrid**
Estadio Vicente Calderón Puerta 25
Merch for the mad.

ARGANZUELA

EL BAR ANDARIEGO

COSTELLO RÍO

PUENTE DE ARGANZUELA

Arganzuela is a hidden gem. Point 1: Madrid Río is the perfect place to get away from the multitudes at Retiro; take a walk, a nap, or a bike ride (picnic included if you rent your bike at Mobeo). Point 2: El Matadero, an old slaughterhouse turned into an incredibly cool theater complex; don't forget to grab a drink in the theater's canteen. Point 3: for those of you who love meat El 7 de Zahonero is the place to go, and Restaurante Peruano Piscomar serves delicious Peruvian food. Point 4: if for some reason you feel like one theater is not enough, Teatro Circo Price and Teatro Cuarta Pared are just steps away from Matadero. Last point: Mercado de Diseño, a fashion market designed to bring together emerging designers from all over the world. Can you tell Arganzuela is trying to become Madrid's next hipster spot? Point taken.

TEATRO CIRCO PRICE

PUERTA DE LA TOLEDO
(5)

JARDIN
DEL RASTRO

18

RONDA DE VALENCIA

16

EMBAJADORES
(3)

CALLE DE SEBASTIÁN ELCANO

CALLE DE TOLEDO

PASEO DE LOS OLMOS

8

CALLE DE SAN
ISIDORO DE
SEVILLA

PASEO DE LAS ACACIAS

CALLE DE ERCILLA

14

11

CALLE DEL
LABRADOR

PASEO DE SANTA MARÍA DE LA CABEZA

CALLE DE LA BATALLA
DEL SALADO

17

PIRÁMIDES
(5)

PASEO DEL DR. VALLEJO NAGERA

PASEO DE LA ESPERANZA

CALLE FERROCARRIL

JARDIN
CONCHA PIQUER

7

GLORIETA DE LAS PIRÁMIDES

CALLE DE ARGANDA

CALLE DE ARGANDA

PLAZA
DE LAS
PEÑUELAS

15

CALLE DEL GRAL.
PALANCA

CALLE DE
CÁCERES

PUENTE
DE TOLEDO

5

4

MADRID
RIO

PASEO DE LAS YESERÍAS

PLAZA
GRAL. MAROTO

CALLE FERNANDO POO

CALLE DE JAIME EL CONQUISTADOR

CALLE DE EMBAJADORES

PASEO DE LAS DELICIAS

RÍO MANZANARES

CALLE DE ANTONIO LÓPEZ

PASEO DE LA CHOPERA

9

6

13

10

2

1

3

19

12

20

RÍO MANZANARES

LEGAZPI
(3) (6)

ARGANZUELA

LANDMARKS

Centro Cultural de la Casa del Reloj
Paseo de la Chopera 6
Cultural center on the inside, beautiful building on the outside.

Invernadero del Palacio de Cristal de Arganzuela
Paseo de la Chopera 10
Not as impressive as the one in Retiro, but still worth a visit.

Matadero
Paseo de la Chopera 14
Old slaughterhouse turned into theater complex. Just great.

Madrid Río
Puente de Toledo
Madrid's other signature park besides Retiro.

Puente Monumental de Arganzuela
Paseo de las Yeserías 19
Just a very cool bridge.

RESTAURANTS

Costello Río
Plaza Gral. Maroto 4
Great burger joint next to Matadero.

El 7 de Zahonero
Paseo de las Yeserías 7
If you're feeling particularly carnivorous. As we usually are.

Restaurante Peruano Piscomar
Calle de San Isidoro de Sevilla 4
One of Madrid's best Peruvian restaurants, hands-down.

Trattoria Increscendo
Calle de Jaime el Conquistador 31
Traditional Italian that won't break your wallet.

Venta Matadero
Paseo de la Chopera 43
Tapas and wine, wine and tapas.

NIGHTLIFE

11 El Bar Andariego
Calle del Labrador 12
Neighborhood bar, the place to go after a night at the theater.

12 La Cantina Del Matadero
Paseo de la Chopera 14
Canteen inside Matadero, good place to grab a drink.

13 Peña Atletica Legazpi
Plaza Gral. Maroto 4
Another neighborhood bar, this time for Atlético fans.

14 Sala de Teatro Cuarta Pared
Calle De Ercilla 17
Another theater. There's a lot of theaters here.

15 Taperia La Pequeña Graná
Calle de Embajadores 124
You get a free tapa with every beer. For real.

16 Teatro Circo Price
Ronda de Atocha 35
You guessed it, it's another theater.

SHOPPING

17 Chocolatería Valor
Paseo de las Acacias 25
Chocolate con churros, hmmm.

18 Mantequería Andrés
Paseo de los Olmos 3
Founded in 1870, the place to go to buy Spanish products in this neighborhood.

19 Mercado de Diseño
Paseo de la Chopera 14
Fashion market, there's food as well (naturally).

20 Mobeo
Paseo de la Chopera 14
Bike rental shop where you can also buy a picnic basket. We love it.

PARKS &
PLACES

Retiro

asa de Campo

arque del Oeste

arque Berlín

Madrid Río

stadio Wanda Metropolitano

stadio Santiago Bernabéu

aja Mágica

EL RETIRO

RETIRO POND

CRYSTAL PALACE

FERIA DEL LIBRO DE MADRID

Welcome to one of the world's most perfect city parks. Between its well-ordered Rose Garden (La Rosaleda) and the Victorian-era pastorale that's the Crystal Palace (Palacio de Cristal), wandering around El Retiro is a favorite pastime of all Madrileños. No matter which way you turn in the park, you'll run across something interesting, such as the Fountain of the Fallen Angel (El Ángel Caído), perhaps the world's only monument to that nasty boy, Lucifer, or the Casón del Buen Retiro, an annex to the Prado that contains Luca Giordano's unbelieveable ceiling fresco, The Allegory of the Golden Fleece. As with all great city parks, there's a mashup between tourist spots like Retiro Pond (Estanque del Retiro) versus the workaday La Chopera Sports Center (Centro Deportivo Municipal La Chopera), where locals come to work off the hard drinking from the night before. Oh, and don't miss the park's annual book fair, the Feria del Libro de Madrid (usually late May-early June).

ROSE GARDEN

CASA DE CAMPO

LAGO METRO STATION

TELEFÉRICO

LAGO DE CASA DE CAMPO

Oh right--here's the Madrid city park that is the real one, far, far away from the prettified gardens and statuesque statuary of El Retiro. Well, not that far, and 6.8-square-mile Casa de Campo does have three metro stations that service it very well (the Lago Metro Station building is actually one of our favorites in Madrid). There's plenty to do here, from the Zoo Aquarium de Madrid and the Parque de Atracciones amusement park that are great for kids, to paddling around in the Lago de Casa de Campo while waiting for the restaurants surrounding them to open, to riding the Teleférico aerial tram that connects it with Parque del Oeste. Or you can hit some balls at the Centro Deportivo Municipal Tenis, picnic under the trees, jog or bike all over the place, or just find a hill to chill out on and gaze eastward at the city. Perfection.

ZOO AQUARIUM DE MADRID

PARQUE DEL OESTE

TEMPLE OF DEBOD

ROSALEDA

GENERAL SAN MARTIN

Possibly our favorite park in all of Madrid, because the sunset from the top of Parque del Oeste can't really be beat. There's also the fact, of course, that the picturesque Temple of Debod (Templo de Debod) has a commanding presence in the park's southern section; it was installed in the park in in 1968 and donated to Spain by Egypt. The park also sports a giant rose garden, the Rosaleda del Parque del Oeste, and is the base of the Teleférico aerial tram which soars over the Río Manzanares on its way to Casa de Campo. On the park's north side, near the Avenida Séneca, is the "martial" part of the park; be on the lookout for some machine gun nests left over from the Spanish Civil War and an equestrian statue of Argentine hero General San Martín. Viva la revolución!

PARQUE BERLÍN

LUDWIG VAN BEETHOVEN

Yes, Madrid also has a tiny souvenir of the Berlín Wall. It's in Parque de Berlín, a small but beautiful park dedicated to our German amigos. It was inaugurated in 1967, and it has not one, but three monuments dedicated to Germany: a statue of a bear (coincidentally, the bear is the symbol of both Madrid and Berlín), a monument dedicated to the immortal composer Ludwig van Beethoven, and the park's fountain, which consists of three original pieces of what used to be the Berlín Wall- that came a bit later in 1990. Parque de Berlín it's a great spot to go for a quiet walk away from the city center or to relax after a busy day in Chamartín. When the Berlín fountain was inaugurated, an overzealous public employee tried to wash away the graffiti on the wall. Thankfully he didn't manage to, and Madrid got to keep this important piece of history.

BERLÍN WALL

MADRID RÍO

RÍO MANZANARES

PALACIO REAL

PUENTE DE TOLEDO

Madrid Río is that other park, the one nobody talks about because everybody is always talking about Retiro. Which is really unfair, because Madrid Río is actually pretty great. To begin with, it's next to Río Manzanares, the city's one and only river, so the park has great views to three beautiful bridges: Puente de SegoVía, Puente de Toledo and Puente Monumental de Arganzuela. It also has amazing views to Palacio Real and Catedral de la Almudena, if you can find a high enough spot. And if that wasn't enough, it's home to Matadero, an old slaughterhouse turned into a massive theater complex and therefore hipster paradise. Another great thing about Madrid Río is that during summer, the park allows you to use the fountains as tiny swimming pools to escape the city heat. Madrid may not have a beach, but at least it has Madrid Río!

PUENTE DE SEGOVÍA

ESTADIO WANDA METROPOLITANO

Wanda Metropolitano, a football stadium located near Madrid's airport, is now home to Madrid's other local team, Atlético de Madrid. Until very recently, Atlético's headquarters were near the Manzanares river, in the iconic stadium Vicente Calderón, which has hosted not only football matches but also superstars like Paul McCartney and Bruce Springsteen. However, the team has decided to upgrade to an even bigger place: Wanda Metropolitano will be able to host more than 68.000 people, 14,000 more than Vicente Calderón. In order to get all this people to the new stadium Madrid is also opening a new station, Estadio Metropolitano, which apparently will be the biggest metro station in all of Madrid. This all sounds really great, but when will we see this happen? The stadium is supposed to be done by June 2017, but this is Spain and nobody takes deadlines very seriously here, so that could mean anything.

ESTADIO SANTIAGO BERNABÉU

REAL CAFÉ BERNABÉU

BERNABÉU TOUR

Welcome to Santiago Bernabéu, the place where legends are made. Home to historic football club Real Madrid, the stadium was inaugurated in 1947 with the name "Estadio Real Madrid Club de Fútbol", but everybody just knows it as El Bernabéu. It may not be very pretty from the outside, but this place has witnessed some of the best football players and matches in history: Alfredo Di Stéfano, David Beckham and Zinedine Zidane all played here. You can learn all about it in the Bernabéu Tour, an expensive but definitely worthwhile tour which allows you to see the inside of the stadium, the players' locker rooms and the trophy room- Real Madrid has a lot of those. Another great spot from which to see the stadium is Real Café Bernabéu, a coffee place and restaurant with great views to the field. If you want to see a match, make sure you buy tickets well in advance- it gets really busy in here.

CAJA MÁGICA

MAD COOL FESTIVAL

MADRID OPEN

Home to the exciting Madrid Open, Caja Mágica (the Magic Box in English) is a fabulous place to see the stars of international tennis every May--the courts are great and so are the stands, as is, of course, the wizardry of the players themselves (if you're wondering, Spanish grand vizier Rafa Nadal has won four titles here). Unfortunately, the food during the Open is some of the worst in Spain, which is insanely odd, given the fact that during large concert series such as the brilliant Mad Cool Festival (held in July), there is a seemingly unending line of delicious food trucks and beer gardens, but hey--it's a work in progress. Getting here is a bit of an issue given the fact that the stadium is far south downtown along the banks of the Manzanares, though there is a nearby Metro stop (the San Fermin-Orcasur stop on the #3) and plenty of taxis come at the end of the night.

PRACTICAL
INFORMATION

Calendar of Events

Estación Atocha

Estación Chamartín

Estación Príncipe Pío

Driving in Madrid

Metro de Madrid

Madrid Bus System

Aeropuerto Madrid-Barajas

RENFE/AVE

Cercanías Madrid

JANUARY

Cabalgata de los Reyes (Cavalcade of the Magi), 5th of January. The night before kids get their presents, the Three Magi promenade in their carriages around the center of Madrid.
El Día de los Tres Reyes Magos (Three Kings Day). 6th of January. This is the day Spanish kids get their presents, courtesy of the Three Magi. Santa who?
Bendición de los animales en el Día de San Antón (Blessing of the Animals on St. Anthony's Day), 17th of January. Take the animal of your preference (billy goat? Hammerhead shark?) to San Antón church so it can get blessed by a priest.

CALENDAR OF EVENTS

Premios Goya, beginning of February (usually). Spain's Oscars. The ceremony takes place either at the end of January or at the beginning of February, depending on the weather. Or something.

ARCOmadrid Contemporary Art Fair, end of February. Brilliant contemporary art fair featuring tons of European art at the Feria de Madrid. Nice one.

Carnaval, last week of February. It may not be as impressive as the one happening in Venice, but there's a lot of partying going on.

Ruta del Cocido Madrileño, beginning of February and March. During the cold months many restaurants in the city get together to create the equivalent of a pub crawl for Madrid's typical dish, el cocido madrileño. Go to the website by the same name to get registered and have some fabulous cocidos at an amazing price.

FEBRUARY

MARCH

Semana Santa Procesiones, (could be in March or April, depends on the year). The truly impressive ones happen in Andalusia, but you can still see the encapuchados and procesiones (people carrying saints on their backs) here in Madrid. If you're from America, it will wig you out since everyone looks like a Klan member, but it shouldn't be missed. The midnight ones are especially cool.

Ruta del Cocido Madrileño, beginning of February and March. During the cold months many restaurants in the city get together to create the equivalent of a pub crawl for Madrid's typical dish, el cocido madrileño. Go to the website by the same name to get registered and have some fabulous cocidos at an amazing price.

Semana Santa Procesiones, (could be in March or April, depends on the year). The truly impressive ones happen in Andalusia, but you can still see the encapuchados and procesiones (people carrying saints on their backs) here in Madrid. If you're from America, it will wig you out since everyone looks like a Klan member, but it shouldn't be missed. The midnight ones are especially cool.

Feria de Abril, sometime in April. If you can't go to Andalusia for the feria, don't worry, Seville's most important celebration also comes to Madrid. Check out the delicious Andalusian food markets during the day, and flamenco performances at night.

MAY

Madrid Open, early May. See the stars of Spanish tennis descend on Caja Mágica to kick butt on red clay. Viva Nadal!

Fiestas de San Isidro, 12th to 15th of May. Madrid celebrates its patron saint with concerts all over the city and people dressing up as chulapos (Madrid's traditional attire). Enjoy!

Feria de San Isidro, most of May. Madrid also celebrates its patron saint with several corridas in the Las Ventas bullring (dates may vary).

Feria del Libro, end of May and beginning of June. Madrid's most important book festival takes place in Retiro, a fabulous setting for any festival, really.

Feria del Libro, end of May and beginning of June. Madrid's most important book festival takes place in Retiro, a fabulous setting for any festival, really.

Mad Cool Festival, early June. This newish 3-day rock fest at Caja Mágica is brilliant--great line-ups, awesome food options, and music 'till 3 am. Ah, Madrid.

Verbena de San Antonio de la Florida, 13rd of June. Party in honor of Saint Anthony; people dress as chulapos and it's customary for single girls to throw 13 pins in the baptismal font of Saint Anthony's church.

JULY

Día del Orgullo Gay (Madrid Gay Pride), early July. The massive parade celebrating Gay Pride goes through all the capital's main streets.

Veranos de la Villa, July and August. During the evening, the capital's most beautiful and historic streets become concert venues and open theaters to make the most of the summer heat. Just beautiful.

Fiestas de San Cayetano, first week of August. August is the time for Madrid's verbenas (local parties). The first one takes in Lavapiés, and it begins with partying and ends with procesiones.

Fiestas de San Lorenzo, second week of August. This one takes place in Calle Argumosa; local food and local beer in honor of Saint Lorenzo. Gracias.

Verbena de la Paloma, usually around August 15th. The last religious party of the month takes place in La Latina, beginning with a procesión in Iglesia de la Paloma and ending (what else?) with lots of drinking.

Encierros San Sebastián de los Reyes, end of August. If you want to run in front of the bulls in Madrid, this is your chance. Good luck to you.

Veranos de la Villa, July and August. During the evening, the capital's most beautiful and historic streets become concert venues and open theaters to make the most of the summer heat. Just beautiful.

SEPTEMBER

La Melonera, 8th of September. Arganzuela's local party is the last one of the summer. There's concerts, dancing, and, as its name indicates, lots of melons. We love our melons.
Fiestas del motín de Aranjuez, first week of September. This town in the outskirts of Madrid celebrates the Ríot that in 1808 toppled the king's prime minister by actually re-creating that night and assaulting the prime minister's former palace. So much fun.

Fiesta de la Trashumancia, October. One day a year, the cars and people in the center of Madrid give way to flocks of sheep with their shepherds. We're not kidding.

Mercado de El Quijote, 7th to 12th of October. The neighborhood of Alcalá de Henares celebrates Cervantes and Don Quixote every year with a medieval market, theater plays and music.

NOVEMBER

Fiesta de Todos los Santos, 1st of November. For many theaters, it's customary to represent Don Juan TenoRío on All Saints' Day. It's also customary to eat huesos de santo (literally, saints' bones).

Fiesta de la Almudena, 9th of November. Madrid celebrates its other patron saint by offering flowers in Plaza de la Almudena and carrying a statue of the Saint from Plaza Mayor to the Cathedral.

Mercadillo de Navidad Plaza Mayor, most of December. Madrid's iconic Christmas market takes place in beautiful Plaza Mayor. Pick up something for the whole family, and for us, too..

Carrera San Silvestre, 31st of December. Spain's biggest race happens the last day of the year. Because who doesn't feel like running 10 km right before New Year's?

Uvas en Puerta del Sol, 31st of December. People from all over the world come to Puerta del Sol to celebrate the New Year by eating twelve grapes twelve seconds before the clock strikes midnight. Then, the madness begins.

ESTACIÓN DE ATOCHA

ATOCHA RENFE

COMMUTER TRAINS

HIGH SPEED TRAINS

Atocha is Madrid's main railway station. It hosts commuter trains, intercity and regional trains going to and from the South of Spain and high speed trains (AVE) to cities like Barcelona, Valencia and Seville. It is located next to Retiro and Arganzuela, so it's relatively near the center and easy to get to by car or tube (the tube station is called Atocha Renfe and it links with line 1 of the Madrid Metro). Be ready to queue and make sure you arrive at the station with plenty of time. If you're arriving to Madrid Vía Atocha, this is actually a great spot to land: Atocha is near some important Madrid landmarks such as Retiro Park and the iconic Reina Sofía museum. Unfortunately, Atocha is also very well known for other reason: on the 11th of March 2004, several commuter trains arriving to the station were bombed in what constituted the deadliest terrorist attack in Spanish history. A memorial for the 191 victims is in the station.

ESTACIÓN DE CHAMARTÍN

CALVO SOTELO

REGIONAL TRAINS

HIGH SPEED TRAINS

Chamartín is Madrid's second major railway station, located in the north of the city. It connects the capital to the north of Spain Vía regional trains and high speed trains and it also hosts the international train line to Lisbon. High speed lines include the journey Madrid-León, Madrid-Barcelona and Madrid-Valladolid and there are frequent trains to Atocha for all other destinations. Estación Chamartín is further away from the centre than Atocha, but still easy to reach, either by car (Vía Castellana) or by tube (the station is called Chamartín, not to be confused with Pinar de Chamartín, and it links with tube lines 1 and 10). Chamartín is nowhere as busy as Atocha and it has several places to eat or have a drink inside the station. If you have some time to kill before or after your train, Torres Kio and Monumento Calvo Sotelo in Castellana are just a 20 minutes walk from the station.

ESTACIÓN PRÍNCIPE PÍO

CERCANÍAS STATION

BUS STATION

METRO STATION

Estación Príncipe Pío is a railway station that operates as a Metro station, a Cercanías station (the commuter rail service that connects Madrid and its metropolitan area) and bus station. It's located in the area Moncloa-Aravaca and it is one of the busiest stations in Madrid. In the Cercanías platform you can find trains going to the Airport Terminal 4, Alcalá de Henares, or Fuente de la Mora. The Príncipe Pío metro station hosts lines 6 and 10, as well as Line R of Metro de Madrid, a bizarre tube line with only two stations (Ópera and Príncipe Pío). Finally, a bus station is also located within the building with buses going to Casa de Campo, Aluche and other places in the outskirts of the city. Right next to Estación Príncipe Pío you have the old railway station by the same name, a beautiful 19th-century building turned into a mall.

DRIVING IN MADRID

BARAJAS AIRPORT

M30

GRAN VÍA

Surprisingly pleasant and easy, for the most part, as long as you're not in a hurry, that is. The highways can be a nightmare during commuting times, as can the Gran Vía on a Friday night, but zipping around otherwise isn't as bad as you might think (the Madrileños might disagree, except for the ones who've had to sit in traffic in, say, New York or New Delhi). If you want to drive around the historic center, however, we suggest getting the smallest car possible, since both the streets and the parking garages that are underneath require very good depth perception (and excellent parking skills). The M30 is the ring highway with plenty of places to either enter the city or escape it, as the case may be; with no traffic, Barajas Airport is a mere thirty minutes east of the city taking either the A2 or the A3.

METRO DE MADRID

SPORTS STADIUMS

PACO DE LUCÍA

BARAJAS AIRPORT

An absolutely perfect little transit system, the Madrid Metro pretty much goes anywhere you need it to, including three stops in Casa de Campo, stations right by all the major sports stadiums, and, of course, it's direct to Barajas Airport. 12 lines and a nearly 300 stations (with more being built every day) run higgledy-piggledy under Madrid's streets, but once you're down there, the connections and maps are easy as pie. Unfortunately for all the late-night carousers in Malasaña and Chueca, the metro stops at 1:30 am and doesn't re-open until 7 am. You can buy single-ticket rides, a 10-ride ticket, and, if you're planning on spending months or years here, there is a monthly pass (TTP card) that's worth the two trips to the government office to figure it out (you can try doing it online, but….good luck). The newer stations, like Paco de Lucía in the north, are quite stunning (as are the mountains when you get outside!).

CASA DE CAMPO

MADRID BUS SYSTEM

ESTACIÓN SUR DE MADRID

NIGHT BUSES

10-RIDE TICKET METROBUS

Most Madrileños travel either by car or tube, but Madrid also has a fantastic bus system to move around the city. A single ticket is €1.50 (you can buy it on the bus itself) but if you're going to travel a lot we recommend getting the 10-ride ticket Metrobus, which you can get on any metro station and can be used for both the bus and the metro. Most buses operate only during the day, but night owls can also use the night buses (which are also known as owls), although you might find yourself waiting 30 minutes or even an hour for your bus to arrive. If you want to travel to the outskirts of the city, the bus is your best option, since it reaches some of the further away neighborhoods that the metro hasn't gotten to yet. You can also travel all around Spain by bus: Madrid's long distance bus stations, Estación Sur de Madrid and Estación de Avenida de América, will take you almost anywhere you want.

AVENIDA DE AMÉRICA

AEROPUERTO MADRID-BARAJAS

ANTONIO LAMELA

TERMINAL 4

RICHARD ROGERS

Aeropuerto Adolfo Suárez Madrid-Barajas--better known as just Barajas--has four terminals (all connected by metro) so make sure to check which one your airline departs from! The first three terminals are relatively small and unimpressive, but Terminal 4 is just a modern masterpiece--its open-air design, colorful pillars, and easy multi-level access between gates, baggage, ground transportation, and the Metro should be something that is taken on board whenever a major city needs to redo their airports (hint, hint, New York). The only quirk is that when you get off the Metro, you need to pay an extra fee before you can exit to the gates, but that's about it. Other than that, everything works great, and flying both locally around Spain, as well as taking longer trips, is simply a dream. The food here could use an upgrade, although a MasQMenos will at least provide a decent base of tapas until you can get something better. Architects Antonio Lamela & Richard Rogers should be given kudos for Terminal 4's design, and what's even more remarkable is that an actual government signed off on it. So: well done, Spain.

MASQMENOS

RENFE/AVE

PAMPLONA

MÁLAGA

BARCELONA

AVE (Alta Velocidad Española) is the high speed rail service operated by Renfe, Spain's main railway company. Thanks to this train service you can travel from Madrid to Barcelona in just 2 hours and 30 minutes, 3 hours if it stops at some stations along the way. Other destinations available from Madrid stations (either Atocha or Chamartín) are Sevilla, Valencia, Valladolid, León, Málaga, Huesca, Albacete, Alicante, SegoVía, and hopefully Galicia from 2018 onwards. Renfe's other high speed rail service, called Alvia, is not as fast as AVE but still operates at the more than acceptable speed of 250km per hour. Some destinations available from Madrid in this service are Bilbao, Cádiz, Gijón, Huelva, Logroño, Pamplona, Santander, Castellón and Vitoria. Both train services are comfortable and reliable, at least most of the time. Definitely the best way to travel quickly around Spain.

BILBAO

CERCANÍAS MADRID

GUADALAJARA

ARANJUEZ

EL ESCORIAL

Cercanías, the commuter rail service that connects Madrid to its greater metropolitan area, is also operated by Renfe (surprise, surprise). Most people that don't live in the city use this service to commute to work, since Cercanías has 89 stations that reach most major commuter hubs in the province of Madrid. Many of Madrid's major train stations, such as Atocha, Chamartín, Nuevos Ministerios, and Sol, are also connected to the Madrid Metro system, so that's of course handy for winding up, Vía train, exactly where you need to be. Madrid has some beautiful towns in the outskirts of the city, so if you want to visit them (and you should!) Cercanías is your best choice. We recommend Guadalajara, Aranjuez or El Escorial, but these are just some of the available destinations. Trains operate frequently from 5 am till midnight, and if you're planning to use this service a lot you can buy an Abono turístico, a pass specifically designed for visitors that will allow you to use the service for a maximum of seven days.

ARTS & ENTERTAINMENT

Museo del Prado

Museo Nacional Centro
de Arte Reina Sofía

Museo Thyssen-Bornemisza

Museo Arqueológico Nacional

Museo Nacional de Ciencias Naturales

Museums

Bookstores

Theater

Movie Theaters

Landmarks

Nightlife

Restaurants

Shopping

MUSEO DEL PRADO

GOYA'S BLACK PAINTINGS

LAS MENINAS

FRA ANGELICO

One of the world's great museums, right up there with the Louvre and the Metropolitan Museum of Art. There's a thousand reasons why the lines are as long as they are (get yourself some sort of membership or museum pass, it's worth it), including Bosch's *The Garden of Earthly Delights*, which is one of the most deliciously evil paintings you'll ever get a chance to see. There are several other "El Boscos" to enjoy here as well. Another classic is *Las Meninas* by Diego Velázquez, a brilliant examination of painter vs. subject. The absolutely lovely and vibrant *Annunciation* by Florentine master Fra Angelico rivals any painting in Italy; the Prado's Italian collection also has works by Caravaggio and Andrea del Sarto. Two other must-sees are Goya's *Black Painting series* and the group of large-scale historical works on the first floor, many of which exhibit a level of detail, and a mastery of light, that is extremely hard to pull off in such large-scale works.

MUSEO NACIONAL CENTRO DE ARTE REINA SOFIÍA

GUERNICA

EQUAL-PARALLEL

It's hard to imagine, but the Reina is every inch the equal of the Prado, even though it only covers the last 125 years' worth of world art. Picasso's anti-war masterpiece *Guernica* might be the sole reason many folks visit, but once here, they get to discover the museum's other treasures, including its fabulous collection of 20th-century Spanish painters--there are plenty of works by Dalí, Gris, Miró, Oteiza, and Zobel to enjoy. Its surrealism collection rivals that of the Museum of Modern Art, so you can spend some time with Ernst, Duchamp, Tanguy, and Dominguez while discovering some lesser-known masters as well. The Reina's rotating exhibitions are easily worth a day of their own, since there are three or four happening at any one time, and at least two of them will be giant "career review" shows. Jean Nouvel's stunning addition to the Reina is wonderful, and don't miss Richard Serra's sublime *Equal-Parallel: Guernica-Bengasi*, which has its own room. What a museum.

SURREALISM COLLECTION

MUSEO THYSSEN-BORNEMISZA

HUDSON RIVER SCHOOL

GHIRLANDAIO

RICHARD ESTES

Possibly the single greatest collection of paintings amassed by any one family (we'll give you one guess as to their name), the Thyssen has what seems to be an unending collection of brilliant work since about 1200 A.D., give a take a year or two. Don't come here looking for sculpture, photography, or video work; all that crap? Elsewhere. Instead, just enjoy the masterpieces, such as Ghirlandaio's *Portrait of Giovanna Tornabuoni*, Caravaggio's *Saint Catherine of Alexandria*, Degas' *Tilting Ballerina (Green Ballerina)*, and van Gogh's *Les Vessenots in Auvers*. But don't assume that it's simply a small, well-curated collection of pieces; the collection is VAST and has endless surprises, including (for instance) a brilliant collection of New York Hudson River School paintings to go along with its Renaissance, Impressionist, Cubist, Abstract, etc. masterworks. Even working artists such as Richard Estes and Frank Stella are represented. The Thyssen's outdoor cafe is one of the nicest museum cafes you'll ever see, as well. Astounding.

MUSEO ARQUEOLÓGICO NACIONAL

VISIGOTHIC CURRENCY

ISLAMIC OBJECTS

ROMAN LAW TABLETS

If you've ever wondered about the history of Spain and the Iberian Peninsula in general, even for a second, this place will provide you with the answers. And even if you haven't wondered, chances are, you'll be far, far more interested in history after leaving this place than you were going into it. Everything from original Roman Law Tablets to Visigothic Currency is on display here, and the museum does a fabulous job of curating (and explaining!) its collection of objects, intelligently organized by time period (though it would be fun if sometimes they did special exhibitions that, say, put all the coins, or weapons, or garments, of all the time periods together in one place). Don't miss such treasures as the Mausoleum of Pozo Moro, from 500 B.C., and its wonderful trove of Islamic objects from the Arabic period in Spain. The building itself is the "back half" of the National Library (Biblioteca Nacional de España, a gorgeous classical building fronting Paseo de Recoletos).

MAUSOLEUM OF POZO MORO

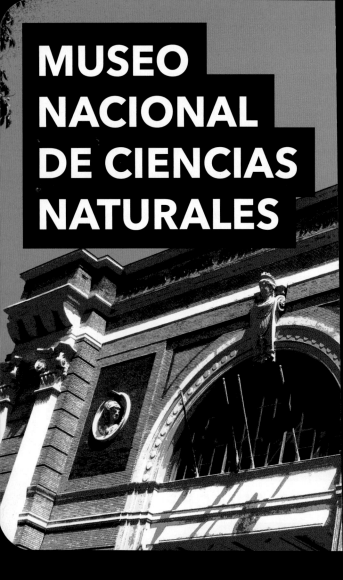

MUSEO
NACIONAL
DE CIENCIAS
NATURALES

Museo Nacional de Ciencias Naturales (Madrid's Natural Science museum) was created in 1771 by Charles II of Spain, which makes it one of the oldest natural science museums in the world. Although it may not be as impressive as the American Museum of Natural History (there aren't any movies about it either) it's still a cool place to visit for all of you science junkies: Museo Nacional de Ciencias Naturales has more than 6 million specimens and historical collections of great value. Some of the museum's most relevant exhibits are a Megatherium (elephant-sized ground sloths endemic to South America) brought from Argentina in 1789, and a Diplodocus, which was donated by American millionaire Andrew Carnegie to King Alfonso XIII of Spain. Make sure you check out the temporary exhibitions as well. The building where the museum is located is also pretty cool and has some awesome views to La Castellana.

MUSEUMS

ART & DESIGN

Well, there's the big three of course: the Prado, the Reina Sofía, and the Thyssen-Bornamisza. The Reina's modern collection is only equalled by the Prado's Renaissance collection and the Thyssen's 800-year span of painting masterworks. But Madrid's smaller art museums and galleries shouldn't be missed, including the green-walled postmodernist Caixa Forum, the Museo Sorolla, the private home of one of Spain's grand masters, the astounding private collections of, well, everything collected by rich dead nobility at the Museo Lázaro Galdiano and the Museo Cerralbo, and the excellent rotating exhibits to be found at the Fundación MAPFRE, the Sala Canal Isabel II (housed in an old water tower), the Centro Conde Duque (housed in an old army barracks) and Salamanca's lovely Fundación Juan March. Ivorypress contains a masterful collection of artist books (though their opening times are typically opaque in the grand Spanish tradition). The murals at La Tabacalera are super-cool, and the outdoor sculpture at Museo de Arte Público are definitely worth a look.

SCIENCE & NATURAL HISTORY

Madrid has a sleeper here--one of the most stunning interiors of any building ever built, housing a lovely collection rocks and minerals. We're talking about the Museo Geominero (Geomineral Museum), in Ríos Rosas, designed by Francisco Javier de Luque; its wood-paneled interior, gorgeous wrought-iron balconies, and stunning stained glass ceiling makes it hard to concentrate on the institute's collection. Also no slouch is the Museo Nacional de Ciencias Naturales (National Museum of Natural Science), first named the "Royal Cabinet of Natural History," in another stunning building just off of Paseo de la Castellana. Tech geeks and scientific instrument fans should love the El Museo Nacional de Ciencia y Tecnología de España (Science and Technology Museum) in the (Metro-accessible) suburb of Alcobendas, while stargazers shouldn't miss the Observatorio Astronómico de Madrid (Royal Observatory of Madrid), housed in yet another amazing building (and containing one of those super-cool Foucault's Pendulums).

HISTORY & WAR

Madrid's excellent Museo de Historia de Madrid (Madrid History Museum), wedged into a classically romantic building in Malasaña, presents a compelling portrait of the city's history; its map collection and period documentation is quite extraordinary, as are the panoramic models of the city itself. Museo Naval (Naval Museum), right near the Prado, has an incredible collection of model ships and covers the history of Spanish sea power. For Game of Thrones fans, the arms and armor housed in the Royal Palace's Real Armería (Royal Armoury) would provide enough props for a full-on battle between the Starks and the Lannisters, while the Museo Arqueológico Nacional (National Archaeology Museum) is the perfect place to explore the history of all the peoples--proto-human, Roman, Visigothic, Arabic, Spanish--that have inhabited the Iberian Peninsula for untold millenia. Its counterpart, the Museo de América (Museum of America) does the same thing for North and South America.

EVERYTHING ELSE

Like every great world city, Madrid's interests aren't restricted to neat little boxes like art, science, and history. Its other museums reflect that range of interests, including the Museo del Aire (AVíation Museum) near Cuatro Vientos Airport, which houses over 150 different planes and flying machines, the Museo del Ferrocarril (Railway Museum), housed in an old train station just south of Atocha, where you can climb through vaRíous rail cars, and the Museo del Traje (Costume Museum), in the University area, housing a wealth of garments from all over the world. Two great children's museums are the Robot Museum and the Museo ABC, both in Conde Duque; don't forget about the museum dedicated to one of Spain's greatest writers, the Casa Museo Lope de Vega, located in (where else but) the Barrio de Las Letras neighborhood. Tired yet?

BOOKSTORES

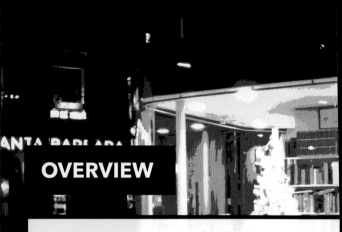

OVERVIEW

There are some fantastic bookstores in Madrid, so whether you're looking for a particular topic or you just want to take a browse, we've got you covered. To begin with, Madrid's most famous book festival, Feria del Libro, takes place every spring in Retiro. This is a fantastic opportunity to expand on your book collection while walking around the city's most beautiful park. Another great place for book browsing is Cuesta de Moyano, which is the name of a hill lined with outdoor booths just south of Retiro. Unfortunately, there aren't many non- Spanish bookstores in Madrid. One exception is Desperate Literature in Calle Campomanes, a small bookstore that prides itself in only selling books in their original language. If you're into rare books, Delirium Books in Calle de Ayala is the place for you, and if you want to learn more about Madrid, head out to Nakama Library in Calle Pelayo.

OUTDOOR BOOKSTORES

We just love the combination of good weather and good books. That's why we love Feria del Libro, the book festival that takes place in Retiro every year from the beginning of May till the end June. During these two months Madrid's most iconic park becomes a sea of outdoor booths where you can find books on almost any topic, courtesy of the libraries and publishing houses that come from all over Spain for this event. If you're lucky, you might even get their author to sign them for you, since many national and international authors come to Madrid for the festival. And if you like old books, make sure you check out El Rastro, the iconic outdoors market that takes place every Sunday in barrio La Latina. There is also a great little outdoor bookstall, Librería Santa Bárbara, on Plaza Santa Bárbara on the Malasana/Chueca border; say hello for us there!

ENGLISH BOOKSTORES

As we mentioned, Madrid is a bit behind other European cities when it comes to English bookstores. However there are still some great ones which are definitely worth a visit. Pasajes Librería Internacional is your average modern bookstore with books in Spanish, English, French, German and Italian, as well as Arabic and Hebrew, so that's pretty impressive. J & J Books and Coffee has books in English and Spanish, as well as good coffee, beer and a lot expats drinking both. And Desperate Literature is just delightful: located in the heart of Madrid, this small bookstore is divided not only into regular sections like English, Politics or Philosophy but also into moods like happy, sad or bored. Desperate Literature also hosts some great chess nights and evening poetry readings. On some nights it's the house policy to give a free shot with every book you buy, so now you have two reasons to buy a book.

SPECIALTY BOOKSTORES

If you're into comic books, we have the bookstore for you: Generación X is the hippest and biggest comic book store in Malasaña, which means it's the best comic book store in all of Madrid. If you're more into photography, fashion or art design, head over to Panta Rhei in Chueca: this bookstore is so cool it even has an Instagram account. Another "cool" bookshop is Ivorypress, a publishing house and art gallery specializing in artists' books; the bookshop is focused on photography, contemporary art and architecture, and design, so basically this place screams art. Another one of our favorites is Delirium Books, a beautiful bookstore that specializes in rare books and original editions. Finally, if you want to learn a bit more about Madrid head out to Nakama Lib in: a lovely little place with a great selection of Madrid-centric books. All the major museums also have great bookshops, including the Prado, the Reina, and the Thyssen.

OVERVIEW

Madrid has a rich theatrical tradition, which over the centuries has produced names such as Calderón de la Barca, Lope de Vega or Tirso de Molina (creator of the immortal Don Juan). The great classical theatres of the capital, such as Teatro Español in beautiful Plaza de Santa Ana and Teatro de La Comedia in calle del Príncipe are in charge of representing these classical masterpieces, so make sure to head that way if you want to submerge yourself in the words of the Spanish literary giants. On the other hand, Madrid also has a "mini Broadway" in calle Gran Vía. It really can't compare to the one in the Big Apple, but it tries--and the view of Gran Vía lit up at night is pretty nice. Finally, head out to the other side of the river to experience El Matadero, an old slaughterhouse which is now a massive theater complex where anything can happen.

THEATERS

CLASSICAL & OPERA

The heart of Madrid's theater scene is its classical theater. One of the city's most emblematic playhouses is Teatro Español in Plaza de Santa Ana. This place has over 400 years of tradition, since it is located in the exact same spot where Felipe II inaugurated an open air theater in 1565. The current building, a neoclassical design built in the 19th century that has the names of famous playwrights written in the facade, is located in Plaza Santa Ana, one of the most beautiful plazas in all of Madrid. Another iconic spot is Teatro de la Comedia, headquarters to the National Classical Theatre Company, located in Calle del Príncipe. Theaters María Guerrero (next to Retiro) and Valle Inclán (Lavapiés) are two other great venues from which to enjoy Spain's classical theater. Finally, it's impossible to not mention Teatro Real, Madrid's main opera house. Located right next to Palacio Real, it's one of the main opera houses in Europe and one of the city's most beautiful buildings (on the inside).

MUSICAL THEATER

We admit it: Madrid still has a long way to go before it can compete with Broadway or the West End, even though the view of Gran Vía lit up at night by the musical theaters in the street is pretty cool. We recommend Teatro Lope de Vega for a musical night; it's where the best shows take place. Other musicals theaters in Gran Vía are Teatro de la Luz Phillips, Teatro Coliseum and Teatro Rialto. Nuevo Teatro Alcalá is also a good place to catch a musical, although it is a bit further away from Gran Vía in Calle Alcalá. If instead of a musical you want to experience a truly Spanish evening, head over to Tablao Flamenco Las Tablas en Plaza de España or Tablao Flamenco Essential in Calle de la Cruz, some of the best flamenco venues in the city. Another very Spanish place is Teatro de la Zarzuela in Calle Jovellanos. This theater specialises in zarzuelas, a Spanish musical genre that combines popular songs and dance..

EL MATADERO

El Matadero de Madrid is a former slaughterhouse, located in the district of Arganzuela, which has been transformed into a massive theater complex and arts center. The building, which was used as a slaughterhouse until 1996 and incorporates some Neo-Mudéjar features, is in itself worth a visit, but the truly cool stuff happens on the inside. El Matadero has a space for every artistic expression, such as film, design, architecture and the performing arts. It's theatrical productions in las Naves del Español (the three venues assigned to theatre plays) include the classical Spanish plays as well as more modern plays, some of which may involve the audience's participation (we've warned you). While you're in Matadero, you should also check out The Cineteca (the mecca of documentary films in Madrid), the Central de Diseño (a space dedicated to graphic design projects) and of course the Cantina and Terraza Matadero (who doesn't need a drink after all this art?)

MOVIE THEATERS

OVERVIEW

Spaniards love Hollywood. Hollywood voices? Not that much. Spain uses dubbing for pretty much every single foreign movie, so that can be a bit frustrating for non Spaniards that want to catch a film in Madrid. Fortunately for you, we're here to tell you which cinemas screen movies in their original version. If you actually understand Spanish, or for some weird reason you want to see Alien in Spanish, you're in luck: Madrid has some great venues like Cinesa Proyecciones in Calle Fuencarral and Cine Conde Duque in Calle Goya, where you can catch all the latest blockbusters. Cines Yelmo, next to Sol, screens some movies in V.O.S (versión original), as well as some Spanish movies, in case you want to see what that is about. Cines Princesa and Cines Renoir, both next to Arguelles, also screen movies in V.O.S.

IDEAL

V.O.S

If you want to make sure that the movie you're about to watch isn't dubbed, make sure that the movie title ends with the words V.O.S (versión original). Spaniards usually watch movies in their dubbed version, so most cinemas don't have the option to watch movies in the original. Fortunately, there are some exceptions. Cines Yelmo, conveniently located right next to Sol in Doctor Cortezo, has a good choice of non-Spanish movies in their original version, including the latest blockbusters. On the other hand you have Cines Golem, a modern venue which shows independent movies in their original version. Right next to it are the two other cinemas of Plaza Princesa, Cines Renoir and Cines Princesa, which also show the latest blockbusters in V.O.S. Finally, Cines Verdi, in calle Bravo Murillo, is another great venue with a good movie selection in the centre of Madrid.

LANDMARKS

OVERVIEW

Needless to say, any city that's been continually inhabited for over a thousand years is going to have its share of landmarks and institutions, and Madrid is no different in that respect. World-famous art museum? Check (The Prado). Perfectly manicured city park? Check (El Retiro). Famous street lined with shops, restaurants, theaters, and cultural institutions? Check (The Gran Vía). Famous gathering place for locals and tourists alike? Check (Plaza Mayor, Puerta del Sol, Plaza de Colón, Plaza de España, etc.). Amazingly elaborate City Hall? Check (Ayuntamiento de Madrid). Ancient temple originally from some other place? Check (Templo de Debod). What's fun about this city, though, is that it's got whole classes of landmarks that few other cities have, such as its incredible 46 (and counting) Mercados de Madrid--to wit, the glass-and-iron Mercado San Miguel, the hip Mercado San Anton, and the fancy Platea among them.

Well, there's certainly plenty of these. Like, a million. The big three art museums are of course the Prado, the Reina Sofía, and the Thyssen-Bornamisza, but don't forget about the second tier art museums such as the Caixa Forum, Fundación MAPFRE, and Museo de Arte Público, an outdoor sculpture garden. La Tabacalera is the edgy/anarchist choice for cultural institutions, while the Centro Conde Duque, Sala Canal Isabel II, and Fundación Juan March have much more "official" standing (and present plenty of fabulous art and music shows). The El Matadero theater and arts complex, housed in an old slaughterhouse in Arganzuela, shouldn't be missed, while homage can be paid in person to great Spanish masters at the Museo Sorolla and the Casa Museo Lope de Vega. Madrid's other giant museums, such as the Museo Nacional de Ciencias Naturales and the Museo Arqueológico Nacional, are (very worthy!) full-day adventures.

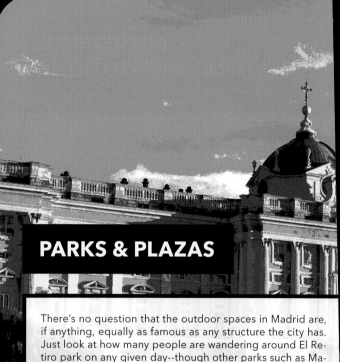

PARKS & PLAZAS

There's no question that the outdoor spaces in Madrid are, if anything, equally as famous as any structure the city has. Just look at how many people are wandering around El Retiro park on any given day--though other parks such as Madrid Río (home to the El Matadero cultural complex), Casa de Campo (with its zoo and amusement park), and Parque del Oeste (featuring the Teleférico cable car and the Templo de Debod) should be explored in detail, as well. The rather barren but still classic Plaza Mayor competes with Puerta del Sol for "largest concentration of tourists in a plaza" honors, but it's the city's smaller plazas, such as Plaza Dos de Mayo, Plaza Chueca, and Plaza de Olavide, where you can find us hanging out with the locals. Plaza de Colón and Plaza de España, by comparison, are just too stilted to be enjoyable for very long.

CHURCHES & ARCHITECTURE

There's nothing quite like the interior of an elaborately-gilded Spanish church to make your jaw drop to the floor, although other cities in Spain, on average, have more amazing structures than Madrid. However, you can't miss Real Basílica de San Francisco el Grande, perhaps Madrid's most famous church. The chapel inside the Royal Palace (itself a structure not to be trifled with) is nothing to sneeze at, either; for something much smaller yet no less baroque, Malasaña's Iglesia San Antonio de los Alemanes fits the bill. One of our all-time favorite structures is the Gaudi-esque Society of Spanish Writers and Editors building, by José Grases Riera, in Chueca, although the Gran Vía sports a delectable number of great buildings along its path as well. For folks of a more modernist bent, Jean Nouvel's stunning addition to the Reina Sofía Museum is a great place to crawl around in--and on top of!

OVERVIEW

As everybody knows, the Spanish like to party, and they sure know how to do it. Whether you're interested in hitting the clubs, finding a cool live music spot or having a beer in one of Madrid's classic cervercerías, this city always has what you're looking for. For starters, the nightclubs: Teatro Kapital, an old theater turned into a seven floors nightclub with a rooftop bar, is one of the city's best known discotecas. If you want to hear some live music instead, head over to Chueca, one of the city's main partying spots, and try El Junco for some of Madrid's best live bands. Malasaña is another great going out place: we especially love the cocktails at 1862 Dry Bar. And what to say about Calle Ponzano in Ríos Rosas, the place to mingle with drunk Madrileños in some of the city's classic cervercerías, such as Cervecería El Doble and La Parroquia de Pablo? Finally, Madrid's roof bars and outdoor terraces are just legendary. We especially love Azotea del Círculo in Calle de Alcalá, an awesome rooftop bar with great views of Madrid.

Madrid has some great discotecas. Teatro Kapital in Calle de Atocha has seven floors, each playing a different type of music. Another classic: the Gabana Club in Calle Velázquez, a nightclub for Madrid's richest and poshest. If rock is more your thing, head over to Independence Club in Plaza del Callao to hear some of the classics. In La Latina, ContraClub in Calle de Bailén and Shoko Madrid in Calle de Toledo offer a great selection of bands and DJs, while Corral de la Morería has some live flamenco nights that you won't easily forget. Casa Patas in Sol is another super-fun spot to experience flamenco, and Café Central is Madrid's premier jazz club.. And you can't say "live music" without mentioning Chueca: Head over to El Junco in Plaza de Santa Bárbara for some great live bands, especially for Thursday's "Black Jam." Just don't make the mistake of thinking that anything in Madrid starts before midnight.

NIGHTLIFE

ROOF BARS & TERRACES

Madrid wouldn't be Madrid without its myriad of beautiful roof bars and outdoor terraces. When the good weather comes, make sure you have a drink in Azotea del Círculo de Bellas Artes in Calle Alcalá, an amazing rooftop terrace with awesome views of Madrid (definitely worth the overpriced drinks). Another great terrace for the summer months is in Hotel Ritz in Plaza de La Lealtad, a beautiful secret garden for the lucky few who can get in. And as every good Madrileño knows, if something can make a rooftop bar even better, it's food: that's why we love the rooftop bar in Mercado de San Antón- excellent food and drinks at an easy reach! Gau Café, a rooftop terrace, bar, and restaurant that overlooks Lavapies from the UNED library, is another good choice. And finally, make sure you go up to El Mirador del Thyssen, a bar-restaurant in Thyssen museum which is only open during the summer months. What a view.

COCKTAIL BARS & PUBS

We just love cocktail bars, and Madrid does as well. D'Mystic in Chueca is the perfect place for before and after additional Chueca adventures, while 1862 Dry Bar in Malasaña is (in our opinion) one of Madrid's most perfect cocktail bars. The Westin Palace in Barrio de Las Letras is another great spot to have a cocktail under one of the most amazing glass atrium roofs you'll ever see. When it comes to pubs, in Madrid they come under two names: tavernas and cervecerías. Although the concept is basically the same, there's one important difference with traditional pubs: tapas must always be had with the beer (after all this is Madrid). Some of our favourite cervecerías are in Calle Ponzano, such as Cervecería El Doble and La Parroquia de Pablo. We also love our tavernas, like Taberna de Ángel Sierra in Chueca (a classic Madrid bar) and Pool and Beer in Chamberí (we just really like the name, and what this establishment is about).

RESTAURANTS

OVERVIEW

Ah, to eat. Do we actually need to do anything else in Madrid, really? (Except drink, maybe…). The food is so good in this town it's unbelieveable, but the irony is that Madrid isn't even supposed to be the center of Spanish Gastronomy. But its wonderfully central location within Spain means that all the great Spanish regional cuisines--Galician, Basque, Catalan, Valencian--are represented here, in its innumerable tabernas, mesons, bodegas, marisquerias (seafood restaurants), asadors (grills), mercados (markets), and restaurants. What's even better is that the food is nearly all good anywhere you go, even to tourist-laden areas like the Gran Vía, Plaza Mayor, and Puerta del Sol. The worst jamon de bellota is still going to be the best ham you'll ever put in your mouth, and we're unconvinced that the Spaniards would ever dare to make a bad tortilla, serve overcooked octopus, or grill a bad piece of fish. So…onward!

SPANISH CUISINE

There are well over a hundred "classic" tapas joints in Madrid that have been serving patrons for a hundred years or more, and we could spend the whole time listing them out--but you can't miss Bodega de Ardosa, perhaps the most classic joint of them all. South of the Gran Vía, El Mollette is another perfect introduction to Spanish tapas as well. For some slightly more modern takes on tapas, try La Pescederia or the excellent Lateral chain. Paella de la Reina will take care of any paella cravings you have, while Asador Real's roasted meats are a classic Spanish preparation. For basic, everyday Spanish food, Meson O'Luar and Los Caracoles are places where you'll be cheek-by-jowl with locals. Seafood is everywhere, just look for marisquerias such as Marisqueria Norte Sur for some of Spain's fabulous grilled shrimp. Basque cuisine should be partaken of often, and the mini-chain El Pimiento Verde has you covered here, with its grilled steaks, rape (monkfish) and artichokes.

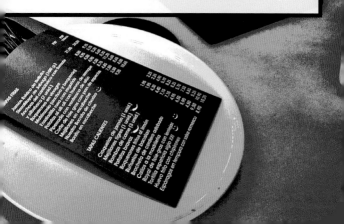

OTHER CUISINES

While the Spanish mostly eat Spanish food, the adventuresome do want to eat other things, occasionally. Some legwork is required to find good examples of other cuisines, but we've got you covered, starting with our favorite Italian place, Bosco de Lobos in Chueca. Chueca also has some good Greek at Dionisos, excellent Thai at Krachai, and delicious skewered Japanese tapas at Yakitoro. When you go to Lavapies, don't miss Senegalese standout Baobab and top-rated Indian Moharaj. Restaurante Omar will satisfy your Turkish cravings, while German brats and schnitzel can be had at Fass. El Cosaco serves delicious Russian food while Malasana's Fondue de Tell is the perfect fondue/raclette joint. Good cheap Pho is on the menu at Vietnam Mekong just south of the Gran Vía. Finally, he double-whammy brilliance of Cascabel (Mexican) and StreetXo (Asian street food) on top of the El Corte Inglés in Salamanca should erase any doubts that the Spaniards know something about cuisines other than their own.

MERCADOS & MISCELLANY

We'd be remiss if we didn't mention some of our favorite mercados to chow down at--including crazy-busy Mercado San Miguel, yet another Madrid classic. If the crowds there get too much, though, check out Chueca's fabulous Mercado San Anton or Malasaña's all-prepared-foods-only Mercado San Ildefonso, one of the hippest spaces in all of Madrid. The upscale-beyond-upscale Platea (in Salamanca, where else?) should be experienced once, as well. There are several areas that are known for lots of great restaurants all in a row, and the best of these is of course Calle de Ponzano in Ríos Rosas and Calle Cava Baja in La Latina. Finally, a shout out to two of our favorite little spots in all of Madrid: the Michelin-recommended La Gastroteca de Santiago, off of quaint Plazuela de Santiago, and one of Madrid's great sleeper joints, El Alambique--seemingly just a small bar in the front, but with big flavors in the back room. Say hi for us.

GAMBAS AJILLO 12€

SHOPPING

FOOD

Well of course we're going to start with food, what did you think? Madrid's fabulous 46 mercados actually have everything you need, honestly--bread, cheese, meats, fish, fruits, vegetables, spices, herbs, etc. and many have a place selling appliances, pots, and pans as well. But to expand beyond the mercados, some of our favorites are Poncelet for cheese, Viena Lacrem and Sugar Factory for baked goods, Taste of America for cravings from across the pond, Santa Eulalia for chocolates, Be Hoppy for beer, Pastafresca for fresh pasta, and Cosmo Cash & Carry for Indian and other Asian products. Supermercado Intertropico has a great selection of Central American and South American products, and Alambique Tienda y Escuela de Cocina has an excellent selection of kitchenware (if you'd like to move beyond the El Corte Ingles experience, that is). Perhaps our favorite gourmet shop of all is the awe-inspiring Mantequerias Bravo in Salamanca--what a shop!

MUSIC & ELECTRONICS

FNAC. Yes, we know, the French giant's store is in the middle of the craziness of the Gran Vía/Centro area, but what can you do? It does have an incredible selection of every type of electronic equipment, plus a decent record shop as well. El Corte Inglés isn't too far behind, either. Shutterbugs will do better at Fotocasion in La Latina, however; it's the best camera store we've encountered in the city. Musical instrument shops are all over the place, from violin shops to African drum shops, but two of our favorites are both guitar-based: Headbanger Rare Guitars in Conde Duque, and the gorgeous Spanish guitars at Guitarras de Luthier. While Radio City remains our favorite record shop, the center of Madrid sports about ten to fifteen different shops, including the underground (literally) Discos La Metrelleta and the always-fun Killer's Discos. Rock on, dudes.

DESIGN & HOUSEWARES

When you're ready to set up shop in a hip Madrid apartment (if you can afford it), chances are, you'll also be able to afford all the fabulous design shops in Malasaña and Chueca, as opposed to just buying whatever's cheapest at El Corte Inglés or IKEA (yes, there is one in the southwest, accessible by Metro). Seriously, just walk around, especially in Chueca-- you'll find them all. Some of our favorite spots outside of this neighborhood design capital are Indigo 50, Passage Prive, and La Recova, all of which are great little shops south of the Gran Vía. Great Spanish leather goods are on display at one of our favorite shops, Taller Puntera S.L., while Papelería Losada Librería Artes Gráficas, in Barrio de las Letras is one of a seemingly unending number of great paper and stationery stores in town--the Spanish love their pens and paper, and so should you!

EVERYTHING ELSE

Clothes shopping is, of course, the personal domain of all Spaniards, so we're not really going to try to suggest places here; obviously, the El Rastro market is a great place for cheap and vintage apparel. Calle de Augusto Figueroa is Madrid's main "shoe street," with about a dozen shops selling everything from fancy moccasins to boots made for walkin'. Salamanca's "Golden Mile" and Malasaña's Fuencarral will also slake your thirst for duds. Beyond clothes, though, Madrid has some great quirky shops that just have to be experienced in person--such as Cacto, the cactus shop in Chueca, Disfraces Paco, La Latina's famous costume shop, Tienda Tintin (you should be able to figure out what this store is dedicated to), Esmalper (toys and figurines), Generation X (comics and board games), ElectricBricks (a LEGO store), and, perhaps our favorite: Fábrica de Cajas de Cartón y Sombrereras--surely Madrid's best hat box store.

LANDMARKS

MAP 1 - MALASAÑA

Iglesia San Antonio de los Alemanes
Calle Puebla 22.
Plain exterior, absolutely stunning interior--worth the euro donation!

Mercado de San Ildefonso
Calle Fuencarral 57
Hip, buzzy night market for prepared foods on three levels--delicious.

Mercado Municipal de Barceló
Calle Barceló 6
Giant 3-level mercado with dozens of vendors-say hello to Marco.

Museo de Historia de Madrid
Calle Fuencarral 78
Fabulous entrance and overall great museum explaining Madrid's history.

Plaza Dos de Mayo
Calle Daoiz & Calle de San Andrés
Where it all went down with the French in 1808.

Plaza de Luna
Calle Luna & Calle Tedescos
Strange brutalist plaza with bizarre plaque that can't be missed.

MAP 2 - CHUECA

Fundación MAPFRE
Paseo de Recoletos 23
Brilliant, rotating art exhibitions--everything from Italian Futurism to modern photography.

Mercado San Antón
Calle de Augusto Figueroa 24B
Best mercado in Madrid--1 floor vendors, 1 floor tapas, 1 floor rooftop bar.

Parroquia de Santa Bárbara,
Calle del Gral. Castaños 2
Looks like an amazing church from the outside...unfortunately, almost never open.

Plaza de Chueca
Sit down and watch the neighborhood move by you (or, more likely, sit and drink with you).

Society of Spanish Writers and Editors
Calle Fernando VI 4
Brilliant Gaudi-esque modernist masterpiece by José Grases Riera.

MAP 3 - CONDE DUQUE

Centro Conde Duque
Calle Conde Duque
Brilliant cultural institution with fabulous rotating art shows and great live music.

Mercado de los Mostenses
Plaza Mostenses 1
Bustling mercado that features a good supply of Asian greens and sundries.

Iglesia de Nuestra Señora de Montserrat
Calle San Bernardo 79
Baroque church on bustling San Bernardo that's worth a peek inside.

Museo ABC
Calle Amaniel 29
Excellent museum of drawing and illustration with a super-cool exterior and kids' programs.

Parroquia de San Marcos
Calle San Leónardo 10
Conde Duque's best church, with an amazing floor plan and ceilings.

MAP 4 - OPERA

Catedral de la Almudena
Calle de Bailén 10
Whacked-out pseudo-modernist cathedral that's one million times nicer on the inside.

Mercado de San Miguel
Plaza de San Miguel
Jammed, but filled with delicious tapas and drinks of all kinds, in all directions.

Plaza Mayor
Barren, cold, devoid of greener filled with tourist nonsense, but still a must; the northern side is lovely.

Royal Palace of Madrid
Calle de Bailén
Giant monument to excess with some absolutely stunning perio rooms and gorgeous baroque chapel.

Teatro Real
Plaza de Isabel II
A lovely experience inside, a bit brutalist on the outside; either way, another must-see.

Parroquia de Santa Bárbara,
Calle del Gral. Castaños 2
Looks like an amazing church from the outside...unfortunately almost never open.

MAP 5 - CENTRO & SOL

Calle Gran Vía
The street of streets. Filled with brilliant architecture and an unconscionable number of tourists

Casino de Madrid
Calle de Alcalá 15
Yup, this is what we consider the best churros in Madrid.

El Oso y el Madroño
Madrid's symbol!

Puerta del Sol
Wall-to-wall tourists attempting figure out where they want to go next, but still an essential stop.

Real Casa de Correos
Plaza Puerta del Sol
The best building to gaze up at i the plaza. 'Nuff said.

MAP 6 - BARRIO DE LAS LETRAS

Caixa Forum
Paseo del Prado 36
Amazing green wall on the outside, fabulous rotating exhibition on the inside.

a Museo Lope de Vega
le de Cervantes 11
homage to one of Spain's
rary giants.

rcado de Anton Martin
lle de Santa Isabel 5
stling as all other mercados,
at beer shop inside.

seo Nacional Centro de Arte
na Sofía
le de Santa Isabel 52
e pillar of Madrid's triumvirate
world-class museums; this is
modern stuff.

seo Thyssen-Bornemisza
seo del Prado 8
other pillar, and possibly the
rld's greatest privately-held
lections of paintings

rcado de San Miguel
za de San Miguel
mmed, but filled with delicious
as and drinks of all kinds, in all
ections.

AP 7 - LAVAPIES & EMBAJADORES

blioteca Escuelas Pías
lle del Sombrerete 15
rmer hermitage brilliantly trans-
rmed into a library for UNED.

Rastro
za de Cascorro
adrid's most famous street
arket, every Sunday until your
ad explodes.

Tabacalera
lle de Embajadores 53
rmer tobacco factory turned
rmal/informal artist studios &
rformance spaces. Funky.

ercado San Fernando
lle de Embajadores 41
rilliant mercado with lots of
uirk, including German beer.

arque Casino de la Reina
lle de Embajadores 68
cals park with yoga, dogs, kids,
d (of course) tables.

Teatro VALLE-INCLÁN
Calle de Valencia 1
Super-cool modern theater and
home to the Centro Dramático
Nacional.

MAP 8 - LA LATINA

Plaza de la Paja
Madrid as it was during the reign
of the Austrias. A hidden gem.

Mercado de la Cebada
Plaza de la Cebada
Giant (and we mean giant) merca-
do that has the craziest roof ever.

Puerta de Toledo
Glorieta Puerta de Toledo
Famous portal, one of nineteen
original gates to the city.

**Real Basílica de San Francisco
el Grande**
Calle San Buenaventura 1
The granddaddy of Madrid
churches. Great back rooms, too.

Teatro La Latina
Plaza de la Cebada 2
Classic Madrid theater presenting,
well, the classics.

MAP 9 - ARGÜELLES

Museo Cerralbo
Calle Ventura Rodríguez 17
Private collection of everything
by the Marquis of Cerralbo.
Awesome.

Plaza de España
Gathering place of all sorts of
folks, with empty Edificio España
looming over it all. Nice fountain.

Estación de Príncipe Pío
Paseo de la Florida 2
Huge light-filled train station/mall
with in-house movie theater.

Teleférico de Madrid
Paseo del Pintor Rosales
Soar over Madrid in an aerial tram
on your way to adventures in
Casa de Campo.

Templo de Debod
Parque del Oeste
One of Madrid's classic attractions, with a killer overlook to
boot. Classic Madrid theater
presenting, well, the classics.

MAP 10 - CHAMBERÍ WEST

Arco de la Victoria
Av. Arco de la Victoria
We won! We won! Whatever
it was…

Faro de Moncloa
Av. Arco de la Victoria 2
Cool observation deck but the
Teleférico is cooler.

Museo de América
Av. de los Reyes Católicos 6
We came, we saw, we con-
quered…

**Parroquia del Santísimo Cristo
de la Victoria**
Calle de Fernando el Católico 45
With a name this long, it's got to
be important.

**Parroquia de San Cristobal
and San Rafael**
Calle de Bravo Murillo 39
See above.

MAP 11 - CHAMBERÍ EAST

Basilica Parroquia La Milagrosa
Calle de García de Paredes 45
Just another amazing Spanish
church.

**Colegio de Ingenieros de Cami-
nos, Canales y Puertos**
Calle de Almagro 42
One of the most beautiful buildings in Madrid.

Galería Marlborough
Calle de Orfila 5
Great, modern gallery--always
something to argue over, at least.

LANDMARKS

Museo Sorolla
Paseo del General Martínez Campos 37
Pay homage to the master; nice back garden.

Parroquia San Fermín de los Navarros
Paseo de Eduardo Dato 10
A bit brutalist on the outside, more than beautiful inside.

Plaza de Olavide
One of the most perfectly-designed public spaces on Planet Earth. Promise.

MAP 12 - SALMANCA

Fundación Juan March
Calle de Castelló 77
All brilliant here--exhibits, shop, garden, performance spaces.

Museo Arqueológico Nacional
Calle de Serrano 13
Possibly one of the best archeology museums in the world. Awesome.

Museo de Arte Público
Paseo de la Castellana 40
Outdoor sculpture park under a bridge. Sublime.

Museo Lázaro Galdiano,
Calle de Serrano 122
Very old books. We mean VERY old books. And a Bosch. Crazy.

Parroquia de San Manuel y San Benito
Calle de Alcalá 83
Giant church across the street from Retiro Park. Stunning mosaics.

MAP 13 - EL RETIRO & IBIZA

Ayuntamiento de Madrid
Plaza Cibeles 1A
Madrid's unbelievably ornate city hall, with an observatory at the top.

Museo Nacional del Prado
Paseo del Prado
The mothership. All the guys are here--Goya, Velázquez, El Bosco, Ribera...those guys.

Museo Naval
Paseo del Prado 5
Awesome Naval museum with amazing models and generally cool exhibits.

Observatorio Astronómico de Madrid
Calle de Alfonso XII
You won't see much of the stars, but the telescopes are neat.

Palacio de Cristal
Paseo República de Cuba 4
One of Retiro's most famous sights; the art inside is curated by the Reina.

Puerta de Alcalá
Famed in story and song, but not all that impressive.

Real Jardín Botánico
Plaza de Murillo 2
Stunning (though not free) botanic garden steps from the Prado and Retiro.Awesome.

MAP 14 - RÍOS ROSAS

Hospital de Jornaleros de Maudes
Calle de Maudes 17
Yes, it really is a hospital. Weird but pretty.

Museo Geominero
Calle de Ríos Rosas 23
Cool geological museum with absolutely stunning interior.

Nuevos Ministerios
Paseo de la Castellana
Hulking, sprawling government complex everyone tries to avoid.

Sala Canal de Isabel II
Calle Santa Engracia 125
Old circular water plant now converted into brilliant art exhibition space.

Santa Maria del Silencio
Calle de Raimundo Fernández Villaverde 18A
Sssshhh...quiet

MAP 15 - CUATRO CAMINOS

Plaza de Azca
Paseo de la Castellana
Decent enough outdoor space, sometimes (thankfully) filled with food trucks.

Parroquia San Antonio de Cuatro Caminos
Calle de Bravo Murillo 150
Yet another Spanish church, this one dedicated to Saint Anthony.

Torre Picasso
Plaza Pablo Ruiz Picasso
One of Madrid's skyscrapers. Skip it, get some tapas instead.

MAP 16 - EL VISO & CASTELLANA

AuditoRío Nacional de Música
Calle del Príncipe de Vergara 146
Madrid's main concert hall for classical music.

Museo Nacional de Ciencias Naturales
Calle de José Gutiérrez Abascal 2
Giant, sprawling, amazing.

Plaza de la República Argentina
The dolphins in the fountain are pretty cute, we think.

MAP 17 - CHAMARTÍN

Centro de Exposiciones Arte Canal
Paseo de la Castellana 214
Former canal management space turned into rotating art exhibitions; nice one.

Bernabéu Tour
Paseo de la Castellana 142
Live the dream.

Estadio Santiago Bernabéu
Paseo de la Castellana 142
The mothership of Spanish soccer. Ugly outside, magic inside.

Palacete de los Duques de Pastrana
Paseo de la Habana 208
Dead duke's digs; now an event space.

Plaza Castilla
Weird-ass sculpture from Calatrava. You can't win them all.

MAP 18 - TETUÁN

Palacio de Congresos de Madrid
Paseo de la Castellana 99
Giant exposition hall for, well, giant expositions.

Museo Tiflológico (ONCE)
Calle la Coruña 18
Art, sculpture, and materials museum dedicated to the blind; very cool.

MAP 19 - VICENTE CALDERÓN

Río Manzanares
It's tiny, but it's the city's only river. What can you do.

Parque de San Isidro
Great park on the other side of the river, check out the ermita (hermitage) in honour of the saint.

Puente de Andorra
Cool three-pronged footbridge over the mighty Manzanares.

Puente de SegoVía
Madrid's oldest bridge, if you're into bridges. Which you should be.

Puente de Toledo
300-year-old baroque bridge by Pedro de Ribera. Check it out.

MAP 20 - ARGANZUELA

Centro Cultural de la Casa del Reloj
Paseo de la Chopera 6
Cultural center on the inside, beautiful building on the outside.

Invernadero del Palacio de Cristal de Arganzuela
Paseo de la Chopera 10
Not as impressive as the one in Retiro, but still worth a visit.

Matadero
Paseo de la Chopera 14
Old slaughterhouse turned into theater complex. Just great.

Madrid Río
Puente de Toledo
Madrid's other signature park besides Retiro.

Puente Monumental de Arganzuela
Paseo de las Yeserías 19
Just a very cool bridge. What, no El Greco paintings?

NIGHTLIFE

MAP 1 - MALASAÑA

1862 Dry Bar
Calle del Pez 27
Perfect cocktails in one of Madrid's most perfect cocktail bars. Enjoy.

Fábrica Maravillas
Calle de Valverde 29
Malasaña's own microbrewery, designed to look like a Danish coffee shop. Bizarre.

Harvey's Cocktail Bar
Calle Fuencarral 70
Designed like a Vegas or L.A. lounge, good drinks, decent food too.

The Stuyck Co
Calle Corredera Alta de San Pablo 33
Rotating menu of on-tap craft beers, plus (of course) stuff to nosh on.

MAP 2 - CHUECA

D'Mystic
Calle de Gravina 5
Perfect Madrid cocktail bar for before and after additional Chueca adventures.

El Junco
Plaza de Sta. Barbara 10
Head over at midnight for some of Madrid's best live bands, especially
Thursday's "Black Jam."

Tony2
Calle del Almirante 9
Only if you feel like singing karaoke next to a grand piano surrounded by drunk Spanish people.

Taberna de Ángel Sierra
Calle de Gravina 11
Classic Madrid bar that you need to drink a beer in, sometime..

MAP 3 - CONDE DUQUE

Bodegas El Maño
Calle de la Palma 64
Hundred-year-old bodega serves up drinks late into the night. Ah, Madrid.

El Jardín Secreto
Calle Conde Duque 2
Yes, it's a restaurant, but the decor is trippy enough for, well, you know…

Jack Percoca
Calle Conde Duque 14
It's a little bit of everything. Including cocktails.

Palma Brew
Calle de la Palma 50
Cool beer shop with (what else?) in-store tastings.

Tempo Club
Calle Duque de Osuna 8
Hippest spot in the 'Duque. Live music, DJs, stiff drinks.

MAP 4 - OPERA

Anticafé
Calle Unión 2
A little bit of everything, but that includes alcohol.

Beer Station
Cuesta Santo Domingo 22
We know what pulls into this station, and we're taking that train.

The Hat Madrid
Calle Imperial 9
Super-cool top floor bar of the Hat Hotel. No bling, just cool.

Los Amigos
Calle de las Conchas 6
Wanna go drink with the locals? Here 'tis.

MAP 5 - CENTRO & SOL

Café Central
Plaza del Ángel 10
One of the best venues for jazz in the entire solar system, hands-down.

Casa Patas
Calle Cañizares 10
Super-fun, super-classic spot to experience flamenco. A must.

Cervecería Alemana
Plaza Sta. Ana 6
Because beer from Germany tastes good, no matter where you are.

El Sol
Calle Jardínes 3
Madrid's most classic of all its classic rock clubs. Nice one.

Independance Club
Plaza del Callao 4
If you enjoy classic rock music, this is the nightclub for you. Also your chance to discover some Spanish rock.

MAP 6 - BARRIO DE LAS LETRAS

Azotea del Círculo
Calle de Alcalá 42
See Madrid (especially the east) from the top of this awesome rooftop bar.

La Venencia
Calle Echegaray 7
Old-timey bar on a narrow street what can be bad?

Teatro Kapital
Calle de Atocha 125
Madrid's biggest nightclub: it only has seven floors.

The Westin Palace
Plaza de las Cortes 7
Have a cocktail under one of the most amazing glass atrium roofs you'll ever see.

MAP 7 - LAVAPIES & EMBAJADORES

Gau Cafe
Calle Tribulete 14
Rooftop terrace, bar, and restaurant that overlooks Lavapies from the UNED library. A must.

Gato Verde
lle de la Torrecilla del Leal 15
a of good beers late into the
ht. As it should be.

Fantástica de Lavapiés
le de Embajadores 42
u want locals? Here they are.

Huelga de Lavapiés
lle Zurita 39
pers and supplies for all those
ists who can't afford Las Letras.

MAP 8 - LA LATINA

aravan Cocktail Bar
le Príncipe Anglona 3
e have tried many cocktail bars
Madrid, and we like them all.

ontraClub
lle de Bailén 16
ockin' (live music, DJs) club steps
f Madrid's most classic church.
f course.

orral de la Morería Restaurant
alle de la Morería 17
ve flamenco and dead flesh
erved in classic surroundings.

uana La Loca
laza Puerta de Moros 4
ipster Madrid pintxos bar, and
ice-versa.

hoko Madrid
alle de Toledo 86
arger live music club with good
otating mix of artists.

MAP 9 - ARGÜELLES

Casa Paco
Calle Juan Álvarez Mendizábal 85
ortillas and cervezas in a classic
Madrid joint.

Cines Golem
Calle de Martín de los Heros 14
One of three great movie theaters
n Plaza Princesa.

Cines Princesa
Calle de la Princesa 3
The mothership of Madrid movie
theaters. 14 screens.

Cines Renoir
Calle de Martín de los Heros 12
The arthouse portion of the
Renoir juggernaut.

Tablao Flamenco Las Tablas
Plaza de España 9
Classic flamenco steps from, well,
everything.

MAP 10 - CHAMBERÍ WEST

Pool and Beer
Calle de Joaquín María López 17
We are completely in agreement
with the ethos of this
establishment.

Sala Berlanga
Calle de Andres Mellado 53
Movie house with film festivals
and more.

Teatros de Canal
Calle de Cea Bermúdez 1
One of the centers of the Madrid
performing arts scene.

Teatro Galileo
Calle de Galileo 39
Theater for all, music for some.

MAP 11 - CHAMBERÍ EAST

Bar Méntrida
Plaza de Olavide 3
One of several options for drinks
on the plaza.

Cines Verdi
Calle Bravo Murillo 28
One of the few cinemas in Madrid
that screens movies in their
original version.

Teatros Luchana
Calle de Luchana 38
A mix of family and adult theater,
some concerts.

Whitby
Calle de Almagro 22
We don't know why we like to
drink here, we just do. And we do.

MAP 12 - SALMANCA

Arts Club Madrid
Calle de Velázquez 96
Hipper than thou, but go once
anyway. Also plenty of food (it's
Madrid, after all).

Gabana Club
Calle de Velázquez 6
THE posh nightclub in Madrid.

Cofradía M.A.D
Calle de Juan Bravo 57
A dive bar in a rich neighbor-
hood! We're MAD for it.

The Geographic Club
Calle de Alcalá 141
Sip cocktails and feel like an
explorer while surrounded by
objects from all over the world.

TATEL Madrid
Paseo de la Castellana 36
Uber-hip joint owned by athletes
serving cocktails that smoke and
stuff like that. Go once. But go.

MAP 13 - EL RETIRO & IBIZA

Bar Martín
Av. de Menéndez Pelayo 17
Classic Madrid watering hole
across the street from Retiro.

Cine Renoir Retiro
Calle de Narváez 42
Fresh flicks from the Renoir folks.
Fabulous.

Hotel Ritz Terrace
Plaza de la Lealtad 5
Well, of course. Gin tonic, por
favor.

MAP 14 - RÍOS ROSAS

Cervecería El Doble
Calle de Ponzano 17
Because two beers are better
than one, silly, of course.

Cine Conde Duque Santa Engracia
Calle Santa Engracia 132
Catch a flick and then go eat on Calle de Ponzano.

La Máquina Chamberí
Calle de Ponzano 39
This is a perfect machine; bar in front, restaurant in back.

La Parroquia de Pablo
Calle de Breton de los Herreros 16
Because everyone should have their own church, including Pablo.

Santa Teresa Shop
Calle de Ponzano 93
Gazpacho cocktails? Why not?

MAP 15 - CUATRO CAMINOS

Discoteca Tartufo
Calle de Hernani 75
If you must dance in this neighborhood, this is the place.

El Quinto Vino
Calle de Hernani 48
A classic Madrileña tavern. Check out the pictures on the walls.

MAP 16 - EL VISO & CASTELLANA

Casa Puebla
Calle Gutiérrez Solana 4
Perfect pre- or post-match tapas and cervezas near Bernabéu.

El Refugio
Calle San Juan de la Salle 6
For those about to rock.

Fiat Café
Calle de Serrano 197
A fancier bar to watch the match or to listen to some live music.

La Daniela
Calle Gutiérrez Solana 2
Another classic spot to watch El Clasico.

Restaurante/Taberna Cazorla
Calle Rodríguez Marín 80
One of the best Andalusian places in Madrid.

Si Señor
Paseo de la Castellana 128
Margaritas and other less important things on Castellana. Enjoy.

MAP 17 - CHAMARTÍN

Bar La Huella
Calle del Dr. Fleming 4
Next to Bernabéu, perfect place to grab some tapas before the match.

Boom Room (Antigua sala Marmara)
Calle de Padre Damián 23
Nightclub beneath a hotel, only go if you're forty (gasp!).

El Enfriador
Av. de Alberto de Alcocer 47
Be prepared to talk about football.

La Cocina Rock Bar
Av. de Alberto de Alcocer 48
Live music bar; you might also catch a karaoke night.

Realcafé Bernabéu
Puerta 30 Estadio Santiago Bernabéu
Expensive, but you get to see the Bernabéu field while you eat!

Taj Mahal
Calle Bolivia 28
Cocktails and shisha, the perfect way to relax.

MAP 18 - TETUÁN

The Irish Rover
Calle del Dr. Fleming 4
Sumptuously-decorated bar,
great gin tonics.

Gimt
Calle del Capitán Haya 48
Sumptuously-decorated bar,
great gin tonics.

Las Jarritas
Calle de Orense 39
Because every neighborhood
needs (one) sports bar.

La Taberna de Emyfa
Calle del Capitán Haya 11
Every neighborhood needs a
second sports bar.

Moby Dick
Av. de Brasil 5
Great music venue with
awesome decor.

Teatro Gran Maestre
Calle del Gral Orgaz 17
Grand theater, check out its
flamenco nights

MAP 19 - VICENTE CALDERÓN

El Rancho Madrid
Paseo de los Melancólicos 77
Tango nights and Argentinian
meat, and vice versa.

Mesón San Isidro
Paseo del Quince de Mayo 15
Bar and tapas in honour of
the saint.

El Chiscón de la Ribera
Calle San Epifanio 7
Neighborhood bar, we like the
ball pool for kids.

Terraza Atenas
Parque de Atenas
Awesome mojitos in a lovely
outdoors terrace.

Sala Riviera
Paseo Bajo de la Virgen del Puerto
One of Madrid's classic concert
venues.

Sala Trivial
Calle San Ambrosio 8
Liberal club, for the more open
minded...

Teseo Teatro
Ronda de SegoVía 61
Theater nights happen here.

MAP 20 - ARGANZUELA

El Bar Andariego
Calle del Labrador 12
Neighborhood bar, the place to
go after a night at the theater.

La Cantina Del Matadero
Paseo de la Chopera 14
Canteen inside Matadero, good
place to grab a drink.

Peña Atletica Legazpi
Plaza Gral. Maroto 4
Another neighborhood bar, this
time for Atlético fans.

Sala de Teatro Cuarta Pared
Calle De Ercilla 17
Another theater. There's a lot of
theaters here.

Taperia La Pequeña Graná
Calle de Embajadores 124
You get a free tapa with every
beer. For real.

Teatro Circo Price
Ronda de Atocha 35
You guessed it, it's another
theater.

RESTAURANTS

MAP 1 - MALASAÑA

La Bodega Ardosa
Calle Colón 13
The legendary Spanish bodega
that's almost always open (and
crowded!).

La Pesacadería
Calle Ballesta 32
Delicious tapas, ceviche, fish and
meats--try for a table outside.

Lateral Fuencarral
Calle Fuencarral 43
Perfect tapas and great outdoor
tables to rest your post-Fuencarral
shopping feet.

La Fondue de Tell
Calle Divino Pastor 12
Cosy fondue and raclette in the
heart of Malasaña.

El Bosco
Calle Hortaleza 63
Fabulous modernist Italian tucked
behind the School of Architecture; a must.

Dionisios
Calle Augusto Figueroa 8
Perfect little Greek on pedestri-
an-only Augusto Figueroa.

MAP 2 - CHUECA

Krachai
Calle Fernando VI 11
Very good Thai in the heart of
Chueca's hip shopping streets.

Paella de la Reina 39
Calle Reina 39
Classic Valencian paella, but
don't miss the black rice and the
fideos, either.

El Bierzo
Calle de Barbieri 16
Traditional Spanish food at a really
good price.

Tuk Tuk
Calle del Barquillo 26
Great mix of Asian street food
options, especially the Char Siu
and the Rendang.

Yakitoro by Chicote
Calle Reina 41
Skewered Japanese goodness,
plus fabulous marrow and a great
drink selection.

MAP 3 - CONDE DUQUE

Esfahan
Calle San Bernardino 1
Persian goodness in the heart of
Conde Duque. Yum.

Goiko Grill
Calle de la Princesa 26
Hungry after a movie? Grab a
delicious burger. And fries.

La Carbonera
Calle Bernardo López García 11
Cheese and tapas bar.
Did we mention cheese?

Meson O'Luar
Calle San Bernardo 17
Eat classic Spanish tapas with the
hotel workers and cab drivers of
Madrid. Perfect.

Restaurante Peruano Chincha
Plaza Mostenses 3
Good selection of Peruvian
specialties and, of course,
Cusqueña beer.

MAP 4 - OPERA

Asador Real
Plaza de Isabel II
For all your roasted cochinillo and
cordero, in a classic space. Yum.

El Mollette
Calle de la Bola 4
Friendly tapas, especially buzzy at
lunch (2-4 pm, of course).

El Pimiento Verde
Calle Conde de Miranda 4
Escape the madness of the
Mercado and eat fabulous rape
(monkfish) and artichokes.

La Bola
Calle de la Bola 5
Classic Madrid eatery that feels
like home; try the house soup and
gambas a la plancha.

La Gastroteca de Santiago
Plazuela de Santiago 1
Delicious Michelin-recommend
dining on a cute plazuela..

Vietnam Mekong
Calle Isabel la Católica 11
Friendly cheap Vietnamese
escape just a few steps from the
Gran Vía.

MAP 5 - CENTRO & SOL

Chocolatería San Ginés
Pasadizo de San Ginés 5
Madrid's most iconic chocolater
open 24 hours. The place to go
after a night of partying.

Café del Patio
Calle del Conde de Romanones
Friendly, a little bit of everything.

Gourmet Experience
Plaza del Callao 2
9th-floor eatery of the El Corte
Ingles, with killer views.

Lateral Santa Ana
Plaza Sta. Ana 12
Central location of one of Madrid's best small chain of deliciou
tapas joints.

Ateneo
Calle de Santa Catalina 10
Dress-up Spanish restaurant locat
ed in the historic literary building
Ateneo de Madrid.

MAP 6 - BARRIO DE
LAS LETRAS

El Alambique
Calle Fúcar 7
Seemingly small bar hides big fla-
vors served up in the back room.
Mmmm...Argentine steak.

La Anchoita
Calle de Jesús 4
Amazing little seafood-centric
bodega with some of the coolest
bar taps you'll ever see.

El Lacón
*Calle Manuel Fernández y
González 8*
Classic Las Letras spot, love the
decor as well.

Rincón de Esteban
Calle de San Blas 4
Perfect place for Spanish classic.
Enjoy.

La Bodega de los Secretos
Calle de San Blas 4
The secret is out; delicious.

Lamucca de Prado
Calle del Prado 16
Las Letras location of Madrid mini-chain; always dependable.

MAP 7 - LAVAPIÉS & EMBAJADORES

Baobab
Calle de Cabestreros 1
Delicious Senegalese with outdoor seating on the plaza in front. A must.

Dakar Restaurant Senegalés
Calle del Amparo 61
Good local Senegalese for when Baobab doesn't have its act together.

Moharaj
Calle Ave María 18
Best of the Indian joints in Lavapiés, good tandoori of course.

El Cafelito
Calle del Sombrerete 20
The best coffee in Lavapiés, ideal for a lazy Saturday morning.

Taberna Antonio Sanchez
Calle del Meson de Paredes 13
Classic Spanish taberna, complete with boar's heads and wood paneling. Perfection.

La Caleta
Calle de los Tres Peces 21
If you like shrimp pancakes and "pescaito frito" (fried fish) like they do it in Cádiz.

MAP 8 - LA LATINA

Calle Cava Baja
--not one, but 20 restaurants all in the narrowest street possible. Enjoy.

El Capricho Extremeño
Calle de Carlos Arniches 30
Always-mobbed tostas joint worth a stop, of course.

El Cosaco
Plaza de la Paja 2
Russian specialties in one of our favorite 'nabes. Nasdarovje!

Los Caracoles
Calle de Toledo 106
Classic Madrid bar known for its piles and piles of snails. Yum.

Posada de la Villa
Calle Cava Baja 9
Amazing interior design matches classic Spanish cuisine.

MAP 9 - ARGÜELLES

Arrocería Casa de Valencia
Paseo del Pintor Rosales 58
Paella by the park. Go for it.

El Pimiento Verde
Calle Quintana 1
Argüelles outlet of Basque goodness--monkfish, steak, artichokes all delicious.

Restaurante Manolo 1934
Calle de la Princesa 83
Oozing classic Madrid history and cuisine.

Taberna La Charca
Calle Juan Álvarez Mendizábal 7
Lovely interior, good food, perfect for post-Cerralbo analysis.

Tabernícola
Calle de Buen Suceso 20
Beautiful reboot on a fabulous corner location. Ole!

MAP 10 - CHAMBERÍ WEST

Restaurant El Llar
Calle de Fernández de los
Asturian goodness in a nice space.

El Tendido
Calle de Andres Mellado 20
An absolute Madrid classic.

Membibre
Calle de Guzmán el Bueno 40
Delicious corner spot with a few (of course) outdoor tables.

Nakeima
Calle de Meléndez Valdés 54
Crazy-assed, crazy-busy dumpling and tapas spot. Good luck.

Restaurant Tres Bocas
Calle de Gaztambide 11
A bit of everything, just like Madrid. Nice.

MAP 11 - CHAMBERÍ EAST

Burger Joint
Calle Eloy Gonzalo 12
And what a joint. Recommended.

Mandralisca
Calle del Cardenal Cisneros 39
One of our favorite tapas in Chamberí.

New York Burger
Calle Miguel Ángel 16
Maybe not New York, but at least authentically American.

Premiata Forneria Ballaro
Calle de Sta Engracia 90
Utterly stylish Italian with wood oven for 'za.

Restaurante El Mentidero de la Villa
Calle de Almagro 20
Two spaces, stylish, we just like it.

MAP 12 - SALMANCA

Cascabel
El Corte Inglés, Calle de Serrano 52
Skip the lines at StreetXo and eat some of Madrid's best Mexican. Underrated by a mile.

Casa Carola
Calle de Padilla 54
Classic Salamanca joint which you'll realize the second you walk in.

Cazorla
Calle de Castello 99
Classic Madrid restaurant with service to match. Just about perfect.

Lateral Castellana 42
Paseo de la Castellana 42
Our favorite Lateral; tons of outdoor
seating, love the design.

StreetXo
El Corte Inglés, Calle de Serrano 52
Loud, brash, crazy fusion from Munoz. Worth the line once, at least.

MAP 13 - EL RETIRO & IBIZA

La Castela
Calle Dr. Castelo 22
Classy reboot of old Madrid taberna. Nice one.

La Catapa
Calle Menorca 14
Perfect tapas and wines by the glass a block from Retiro; we love it.

La Hoja
Calle Dr. Castelo 48
Awesome Asturian palace of deliciousness; love the interior.

La Montería
Calle de Lope de Rueda 35
Both classic and postmodern tapas. Inventive.

Restaurante Vinoteca García de la Navarra
Calle de Montalbán 3
Fancy Spanish food & wine for a fancy night.

Taberna Arzábal
Calle Menéndez Pelayo 13
An elegant tavern with a great variety of wine.

MAP 14 - RÍOS ROSAS

Atelier Belge Restaurante
Calle de Breton de los Herreros 39
Hip Belgian joint if you need a break from Spanish classics.

Casa Fonzo
Calle de Ponzano 60
Argentinean cuisine. Empanadas a must (of course).

Le Qualitè Tasca
Calle de Ponzano 48
Spanish... with a bit of fusion

Picsa
Calle de Ponzano 76
Because who doesn't like Argentinian pizza?

Sylkar
Calle de Espronceda 17
Possibly the best tortilla de patatas in Madrid. And the best torrijas.

Taberna AliPío Ramos
Calle de Ponzano 30
Hundred-year-old taberna anchoring the gastronomic perfection of Calle de Ponzano.

Toque de Sal
Calle de Ponzano 46
A touch of salt makes everything better, as this fancy Mediterranean bistro will tell you.

MAP 15 - CUATRO CAMINOS

Arroceria Bahía
Calle Dulcinea 65
You should know by now that this means paella. Yum.

Asador Guetaria
Calle del Comandante Zorita 8
Classic Basque joint serving up deliciousness, as always.

Goizeko Kabi
Calle del Comandante Zorita 37
Posh dining but totally delicious.

Lateral
Paseo de la Castellana 89
The furthest north this chain has made it so far; keep going, guys.

La Vaca Argentina
Paseo de la Castellana 87
Dependable-enough steakhouse gracias Argentina.

Marisquería Norte Sur
Calle de Bravo Murillo 97
Delicious seafood, whichever direction
you choose to come from.

Taberna Gaztelupe
Calle del Comandante Zorita 32
The old-world half of the Gaztelupe empire.

MAP 16 - EL VISO & CASTELLANA

Café Saigón
Calle de María de Molina 4
Decent Vietnamese bound to slake hunger after the Natural Sciences museum.

Fass
Calle Rodríguez Marín 84
German all the way, from brats to wurst; also a German products shop.

Hikari Sushi Bar
Paseo de la Castellana 57
Posh sushi bar inside Hotel Hesperia; good for (light) business lunches.

La Ancha
Calle del Príncipe de Vergara 204
Classic Madrid; go for the Armando steak.

Mayte Commodore
Pl. de la República Argentina 5
Madrid's hot spot in the 60s. Ava Gardner was here.

Restaurante Zalacaín
Calle Álvarez de Baena 4
Posh, exclusive...did we say posh, exclusive?

PS Velázquez
lle de Velázquez 136
hizophrenic Spanish diner/shop
ain that has to be experienced
least once.

MAP 17 - CHAMARTÍN

ar La Huella
alle del Dr. Fleming 4
ext to Bernabéu, perfect place
grab some tapas before the
atch.

**oom Room (Antigua sala
armara)**
alle de Padre Damián 23
ightclub beneath a hotel, only
o if you're forty (gasp!).

l Enfriador
v. de Alberto de Alcocer 47
e prepared to talk about
otball.

a Cocina Rock Bar
v. de Alberto de Alcocer 48
ive music bar; you might also
atch a karaoke night.

Realcafé Bernabéu
*Puerta 30 Estadio
Santiago Bernabéu*
Expensive, but you get to see the
Bernabéu field while you eat!

Taj Mahal
Calle Bolivia 28
Cocktails and shisha, the perfect
way to relax.

MAP 18 - TETUÁN

Kabuki
Av. Presidente Carmona 2
Japanese Mediterranean fusion.
Delicious.

Kilómetros de Pizza
Av. de Brasil 6
They're not kidding. Quite good,
nice outdoor options too.

Los Arroces de Segis
Calle de la Infanta Mercedes 109
Perfect paella for patrons of all
places.

Marisquería La Chalana
Paseo de la Castellana 179
Seafooder with large selection of
(different) grilled whole fish.
Nice one.

Mesón Txistu
Plaza Ángel Carbajo 6
Chuletóns, solomillos, entrecotes,
tartars--meat any way you like it.

Ocafú
Calle de la Infanta Mercedes 98
Try the tortilla de Betanzos. You
won't regret it.

Restaurante L'Albufera
Calle del Capitán Haya 43
Fancy paellas in the fancy inside
terrace of a hotel.

Restaurante Reina del Quinche
Calle Tablada 6
Small Ecuadorian place, cheap
and authentic.

MAP 19 - VICENTE
CALDERÓN

Arrocería Imperial
Paseo del Dr. Vallejo Nagera 54
Because every neighborhood
needs a paella place.

Chacón
Calle Saavedra Fajardo 16
Octopus and beer from Galicia
(where else?).

Colombiano La Fogata
Glorieta Puente de SegoVía 1
Great Colombian with awesome
views to Puente de SegoVía and
Palacio Real.

Sal de Hielo
Calle Toledo 140
New hip restaurant with a good
selection of Spanish food.

Mesón A Ría de Noia
Paseo de Extremadura 1
Small and rustic, try the pimientos
de padrón.

MAP 20 - ARGANZUELA

Costello Río
Plaza Gral. Maroto 4
Great burger joint next to
Matadero.

El 7 de Zahonero
Paseo de las Yeserías 7
If you're feeling particularly
carnivorous.
As we usually are.

Restaurante Peruano Piscomar
Calle de San Isidoro de Sevilla 4
One of Madrid's best Peruvian
restaurants, hands-down.

Trattoria Increscendo
Calle de Jaime el Conquistador 31
Traditional Italian that won't break
your wallet.

Venta Matadero
Paseo de la Chopera 43
Tapas and wine, wine and tapas.

SHOPPING

MAP 1 - MALASAÑA

J & J Books and Coffee
Calle Espíritu Santo 47
Books both in Spanish and English, coffee, beer, and expats.

Generación X Puebla
Calle Puebla 15
Probably the hippest and biggest of Malasaña's half-dozen comic book stores.

Viena Lacrem
Calle Sta Brígida 6
Best overall bakery in Malasaña... when it's open, of course.

Panta Rhei
Calle Hernán Cortés 7
One of the best design bookstores anywhere in Spain, and probably Europe. Say hi.

MAP 2 - CHUECA

Cacto
Calle Fernando VI 7
For all your cactus needs. No, really. Seriously. A cactus store.

Calle de Augusto Figueroa
Between Hortaleza and Barbieri.
A dozen shoe shops in a four-block
stretch: paradise!

Nakama Lib
Calle Pelayo 22
Lovely little bookshop with great selection of Madrid-centric books.

Papelería Cámara
Calle de Hortaleza 68
Fantastic paper and art shop for your inner Zóbel.

Poncelet
Calle Argensola 27
A veritable cathedral of cheese for your gustatory pleasure.

Sugar Factory Madrid
Calle Argensola 27
Delectable pastry shop with the best croissants in Madrid.

MAP 3 - CONDE DUQUE

Atticus Finch
Calle de la Palma 78
Best name for a bookstore ever, we think.

Headbanger Rare Guitars
Calle de la Palma 73
Channel your inner Jimmy Page (if you've got the budget).

Pescadería Gonzalo González
Calle Noviciado 9
Great local fish shop if you don't want to deal with the madness of the mercado.

Radio City
Calle Conde Duque 14
Best record shop in Madrid, hands-down. Say hello.

Supermercado Intertropico
Calle de los Reyes 17
Supermarket favorites from all over Central and South America. Impressive.

MAP 4 - OPERA

Alambique Tienda y Escuela de Cocina
Plaza de la Encarnación 2
Great kitchen store, with classes too.

Desperate Literature
Calle Campomanes 13
Fantastic used bookstore with readings and hangouts.

Discos La Metralleta
Calle del Postigo de San Martín 1
Madrid's classic schizophrenic underground record shop; hard to find!

Santa Eulalia
Calle Espejo 12
Absolutely delectable bakeshop in a hip space. Nice one.

Taller Puntera S.L.
Plaza Conde de Barajas 4
You've heard of Spanish leather? This is where to get it. Just lovely.

MAP 5 - CENTRO & SOL

El Corte Inglés [part 1]
Plaza del Callao 2
One half of the mothership--everything except clothes.

El Corte Inglés [part 2]
Calle de Preciados 3
The other half--clothes, toys, extensive basement grocery store.

FNAC
Calle de Preciados 28
French electronics giant's giant store just south of the Gran Vía.

Killer's Discos
Calle de la Montera 28
As opposed to discs for killers. Try it.

Ojalá Madrid
Calle de las Huertas 5
Great women's clothes nearby other good shops, too.

MAP 6 - BARRIO DE LAS LETRAS

Be Hoppy
Calle de Almadén 18
Cute little beer store featuring Spain's ever-burgeoning craft beer scene.

Guitarras de Luthier
Calle Doctor Mata 1
Drop-dead gorgeous Spanish guitar store; drool-worthy.

Indigo 50
Calle de Moratín 29
French electronics giant's giant store just south of the Gran Vía.

Papelería Losada Librería Artes Gráficas
Calle de la Alameda 3
Papers and supplies for all those artists who can't afford Las Letras.

Passage Privé
Calle de San Pedro 8
Antiques, furniture, gifts...just another cool store in Las Letras.

HOPPING

MAP 7 - LAVAPIES & EMBAJADORES

nicería Emilo
e de la Esgrima 12
at local butcher for when you
n't want to (or can't) deal with
mercado.

smo Cash & Carry
e Argumosa 22
rnational grocery store
cking lots and lots of Indian
ducts for home
ry-cooking.

erías Piquer
le de la Ribera de Curtidores

te of antique stores off the
tern side of El Rastro. Slightly
mobbed.

**nda Solidaria Piel de
riposa**
e de Embajadores
ce little non-profit consignment
p. Treasures abound.

MAP 8 - LA LATINA

sfraces Paco
Calle de Toledo 52
ane costume shop that needs
be experienced (once).

Laberinto 2
lle de Carlos Arniches 23
hacked-out antiques shop
uffed to the gills with crap;
esome.

otocasion
le de la Ribera de Curtidores

uper-dangerous camera store
st off El Rastro (so don't go on
unday).

a Recova
aza Gral. Vara de Rey 7
odernist furniture to spend your
rd-earned dollars on.

nderground
alle Bastero 16
ed clothing for the natty
adrileño (all of them).

MAP 9 - ARGÜELLES

Fábrica de Cajas de Cartón y Sombrereras
Calle Juan Álvarez Mendizábal 5
Because every great city needs a great hat box store.

Mercado Municipal De Argüelles
Calle de Altamirano 7
Great 2011 renovation now houses cheery local mercado.

Motor Sport
Calle del Marqués de Urquijo 43
Zoom, zoom. Motorcycles and scooters for hip Madrileños (re: all of them).

Naos Libros
Calle Quintana 12
Killer selection, especially art and architecture.

Papeleria Debod
Calle Ferraz 24
One of a hundred great Madrid stationery stores, it seems. Nice one.

MAP 10 - CHAMBERÍ WEST

Esmalper
Calle de Galileo 27
Toys and figurines for everyone who's into toys and figurines.

Marcial Pons Librero
Pl. del Conde del Valle de Súchil 8
Nice bookshop on the plaza.

Mercado de Moncloa
Calle Vallehermoso 36
Just another perfect Madrid mercado.

Mercado Vallehermoso
Calle Vallehermoso 36
See above.

Salvador Bachiller
Calle de Alberto Aguilera 54
Bags and luggage for the hip set.

Tienda Tintín
Calle Donoso Cortés 20
Yes, a Tintín store. Yes, it's cool.

MAP 11 - CHAMBERÍ EAST

Carnicería Ismael
Calle de Sta Engracia 39
If you can't find what you need at the mercado, there is always Ismael.

Crustó Bakery Zurbano
Calle de Zurbano 26
Fabulous bakery, lovely space. Enjoy.

Mercado de Chamberí
Calle de Alonso Cano 10
One of the grandmasters of Madrid Mercados.

Pastafresca
Glorieta de Quevedo 7
Super-small fresh pasta shop on Quevedo; nice one.

Vino & Compañía
Plaza de Olavide 5
Pretty wine shop on Plaza Olavide; take a peek.

MAP 12 - SALMANCA

Delirium Books
Calle de Ayala 10
Will cause tremors; rare books always do that to us.

Juana Limón
Calle de O'Donnell 15
Friendly juices and pastries from Spanish master Joaquín de Alba.

Mantequerías Bravo
Calle de Ayala 24
Absolutely bang-on French/ Spanish gourmet food/wine shop. Brilliant.

Mercado de la Paz
Calle de Ayala 28
Great mercado with lots and lots of places to buy foie gras (it's Salamanca, after all…).

Platea Madrid
Calle de Goya 5-7
Unbelievably posh mercado with gorgeous interior spaces. Nothing else like it anywhere.

SHOPPING

MAP 13 - EL RETIRO & IBIZA

Cuesta de Moyano Bookstalls
Calle Claudio Moyano
Brilliant bookstalls lining the southern part of Retiro; great finds always!

Feria del Libro
Paseo Fernán Núñez, Retiro Park
Retiro's giant annual book fair is here; totally amazing and absorbing.

Pzes
Calle del Doce de Octubre 11
Aquarium; hey, we're all just little fish swimming in the wide open sea.

Tea Shop Narváez
Calle de Narváez 31
Cutest little tea shop this side of Retiro.

MAP 14 - RÍOS ROSAS

Mercato Italiano
Calle de Ríos Rosas 50
Cute Italian shop/cafe with delicious focaccia, of course.

Pastelería La Maravilla
Calle de Ríos Rosas 41
Not just a pastelería, but also a croissantería!

Poncelet Cheese Bar
Calle de José Abascal 61
The Poncelet cheese masters have added what was missing to cheese: a bar.

MAP 15 - CUATRO CAMINOS

Bicimanía
Calle de Palencia 20
We're crazy for bikes, and so are the Spaniards.

Chocolate Factory
Av. del General Perón 40
The only kind of factory we'd ever want to work in.

El Corte Inglés
Calle de Raimundo Fernández Villaverde 79
In case the one near you isn't enough, here's another.

Ivorypress
Calle del Comandante Zorita 44
Brilliant artist-centered booksh and gallery; sublime.

Mercado de Maravillas
Calle de Bravo Murillo 122
Just another bustling Madrid mercado to love and cherish.

Moda Shopping
Av. del General Perón 38
Giant indoor mall with glass ceiling. Your choice.

Pastelería Mallorca
Calle del Comandante Zorita 39
Perfect pastries for the perfectly dressed.

Zara
Paseo de la Castellana 79
The empire comes to Cuatro Caminos; destroys all pretender

MAP 16 - EL VISO & CASTELLANA

El Miajon De Los Castuos
Paseo de la Habana 19
Pata de jamón, cheese, wine… what else do you need?

Heladería La Romana
Paseo de la Habana 27
Because even the Spanish screar for ice cream.

Retrocycle
Av. Dr. Arce 32
Perfect bike shop with all the accessories.

HOPPING

MAP 17 - CHAMARTÍN

[Ca]stellana 200 - Paseo [Co]mercial
[Pas]eo de la Castellana 196
[Hu]ge shopping complex, you'll [be] lost for hours.

[M]ercado de Chamartín
[Cal]le Bolivia 9
[Go]-to mercado for everyone who [liv]es in northeast Madrid. Great [sel]ection of everything.

[Su]permercados Sánchez [Ro]mero
[Cal]le de Carlos Maurras 2
[M]adrid's fanciest supermarket [cha]in. It even has a terrace.

[PO]LO de UVA
[Cal]le del Príncipe de Vergara 210
[Ju]st lots and lots of wine.

MAP 18 - TETUÁN

Cafetería NEBRASKA
Calle de Bravo Murillo 291
It used to be a classic Spanish chain but there is only one left now.

La Antigua Churrería
Calle de Bravo Murillo 190
Founded in 1913; the churros are still great.

La Papita CRíolla
Calle Pensamiento 1
Colombian coffee place, try the bananas on toast.

Mercado Municipal De Tetuán
Calle del Marqués de Viana 4
Biggest, best mercado in Tetuán. Always a pleasure.

MAP 19 - VICENTE CALDERÓN

Carlos Sainz Center
Calle Sepúlveda 3
One of Madrid's two Kart tracks is in this neighborhood. Run like the wind!

ElectricBricks
Paseo de los Pontones 23
LEGO shop; do we need to say more?

Tienda Oficial Atlético de Madrid
Estadio Vicente Calderón
Puerta 25
Merch for the mad.

MAP 20 - ARGANZUELA

Chocolatería Valor
Paseo de las Acacias 25
Chocolate con churros, hmmm.

Mantequería Andrés
Paseo de los Olmos 3
Founded in 1870, the place to go to buy Spanish products in this neighborhood.

Mercado de Diseño
Paseo de la Chopera 14
Fashion market, there's food as well (naturally).

Mobeo
Paseo de la Chopera 14
Bike rental shop where you can also buy a picnic basket. We love it.

PHOTOGRAPHY CREDITS

Juan Antonio Segal ....
Rociio Montero..
Rubén Vique ....
Robert Photography ....
Courtney Lindeque..
Ricardo Ramírez Gisbert...
Marco Chiesa...
Kieran Lynam ....
M. Martin Vicente ....
Jose A..
Son of Groucho...
Jorge Láscar ....
Ken Marshall ....
Ricardo Ricote Rodríguez ....
Ricardo Ricote Rodríguez ....
Rubén Vique ....
Alberto Cabello..
David de la Mano...
Daniel ....
M. Martin Vicente ....
Daniel Lobo ....
Jorge CG...
bjaglin ....
Olga Berrios ....
Jose Luis Cernadas Iglesias ....
sporras..
Ungry Young Man ....
influenZia marketing..
Carros de Foc ....
M. Martin Vicente ....
Emilio..
Barcex...
thaisa1980 ....
Jose A..
Ronald van der Graaf ....
Ricardo Ricote Rodríguez ....

HOTOGRAPHY CREDITS

golf 124
ank Black Noir 126
.Peinado 128
harik Innael 130
sus Solana 132
uan MaRío Cuellar 134
golf 136
örkur Sigurbjörnsson 138
arco Pagni 140
efan de Vries 142
. Martin Vicente 144
ubén Vique 146
olanda Arango 148
aniel López García 150
aniel Lobo 152
dam Jones 154
dgardo W. Olivera 156
. Martin Vicente 158
athan 160
Mathieu Marquer 162
ric Titcombe 164
araian 166
ason Paris 170
romoMadrid 172
esús Dehesa 174
ary Bembridge 176
talian Lasagna 178